Code of
Conduct

Code of Conduct

Why We Need to Fix Parliament – and How to Do It

Chris Bryant

BLOOMSBURY PUBLISHING

LONDON · OXFORD · NEW YORK · NEW DELHI · SYDNEY

BLOOMSBURY PUBLISHING
Bloomsbury Publishing Plc
50 Bedford Square, London, WC1B 3DP, UK
29 Earlsfort Terrace, Dublin 2, Ireland

BLOOMSBURY, BLOOMSBURY PUBLISHING and the Diana logo are
trademarks of Bloomsbury Publishing Plc

First published in Great Britain 2023

A catalogue record for this book is available from the British Library

ISBN: HB: 978-1-5266-6359-7; TPB: 978-1-5266-7320-6; EBOOK: 978-1-5266-6358-0;
EPDF: 978-1-5266-6357-3

2 4 6 8 10 9 7 5 3 1

Typeset by Newgen KnowledgeWorks Pvt. Ltd., Chennai, India
Printed and bound in Great Britain by CPI Group (UK) Ltd, Croydon CR0 4YY

To find out more about our authors and books visit www.bloomsbury.com
and sign up for our newsletters.

JCƆB

Contents

Introduction
What's It All About?

I stood in Westminster Hall for a few minutes on the evening of Wednesday 3 November 2021. The Commons had voted that afternoon on whether to agree a recommendation from the Standards Committee (which I chair) to suspend the former Northern Ireland secretary, Owen Paterson, from parliament for thirty sitting days for engaging in 'paid advocacy'. Lobbying for a paying client like this is one of the oldest offences in the Commons rulebook, dating in one shape or other back to 1695 and formalised after the cash-for-questions scandal in the 1990s (see pp. 184–6). But despite being a long-standing senior MP (for North Shropshire) who should have known better, Paterson had repeatedly peddled influence around Westminster and Whitehall on behalf of Randox and Lynn's Country Foods, who were paying him more than £100,000 a year.

The Standards Committee had held a lengthy private session with Paterson a month earlier, during which he was given every opportunity to put his case and was accompanied by his lawyer. We were not convinced by what he had to say and concluded, in a 168-page report which we published on 26 October, that 'this [was] an egregious case of paid advocacy'.[1] Since then, all hell had broken loose. Paterson was touring the corridors and the ministerial offices of the House lobbying MPs for support and denouncing the Committee as a kangaroo court. Every lawyer I consulted told me we had done a thorough job and had given Paterson a fair hearing. Every journalist I spoke to – from every newspaper – thought that Paterson was, in their words, 'bang to rights'. Yet the *Daily Telegraph*, the *Daily Mail* and their Sunday sisters decided to run a vicious campaign seeking to rubbish the parliamentary commissioner for standards, Kathryn Stone, whose memorandum was the basis of our report, as well as the Committee, the parliamentary standards system and me. They had trundled Charles Moore out a couple of times to pen pieces in defence of Paterson. In one, Moore, a peer and a former editor of the *Telegraph*, claimed that 'the hounding of Owen Paterson sets a dangerous precedent in Parliament' because it 'smacks of political revenge'.[2] He presented no evidence for this, but Paterson himself tweeted that this article was 'essential reading'. The commissioner, the rest of the committee and I had wondered whether we should respond but had decided against. Tempers were very frayed by the time we got to the debate, not least because everyone was painfully aware that Owen's wife Rose had taken her own life during the investigation – and had done so on Owen's birthday. Owen claimed she had done so because of the investigation and blamed Kathryn Stone.

The normal process for any Standards Committee recommendation to suspend a member for a breach of the Code of Conduct is that the government tables and moves the motion without amendment as soon as possible. I had presumed that, even though some Conservatives sympathised with Paterson, the government would sit on its hands, watch Owen's friends argue his case and let the

House agree the motion. But the leader of the House, Jacob Rees-Mogg, wanted to protect Paterson. He had raised the case with me in front of officials several months earlier in such a way that I had to write to ask him not to raise it with me again, as it is a breach of the Code of Conduct to lobby a member of the Standards Committee over an ongoing investigation. On the Tuesday morning before the debate, he also told a Conservative Home podcast that he thought the Standards Committee process was defective, because Paterson had not been allowed to call seventeen witnesses, even though they had submitted written evidence, which we were not contesting. Yet the more centrist and pro-European One Nation Tories were said to be planning to abstain and the government chief whip, Mark Spencer, had told his Labour counterpart that the government hadn't decided what to do. When the Standards Committee met that morning, several of the members were very depressed, but I told them I thought the motion would go through 'because the government won't want to be tarred with the brush of sleaze', as I recorded later in my diary.

Late that afternoon the government tabled the formal motion for the thirty days' suspension, but crucially it also persuaded the former leader of the House, Dame Andrea Leadsom, to table an amendment to the government motion which would delay making a decision on Paterson, scrap the Standards Committee and replace it with a special committee with a Tory majority under another Tory MP, John Whittingdale, to consider changing the rules. I was shocked when Sir Bernard Jenkin, who had recused himself from the Committee because he was a close friend of Paterson, collared me in the Library corridor and showed me the amendment. 'Utterly corrupt,' I said. It sought to change the rules to protect a named individual at the very last moment in the disciplinary process. As I wrote in my diary that night, 'it moved the goalposts after the shooter had kicked the ball'. That was the kind of thing you might expect in Russia or China, but not in Britain. I was so furious I went for a run, to Tower Bridge and back, roughly seven miles. I was listening to U2 and Bonnie Tyler, but the music kept on being interrupted by journalists phoning me for a comment, which wound me up so much as I had gone for a run deliberately to avoid journalists that I did my fastest time for ages.

Back in the Commons, I found the government whips were scrabbling around trying to get Tory MPs to sign the amendment. The whole government – and therefore Prime Minister Boris Johnson and Downing Street – was tearing up the rulebook to protect Paterson. Tory MPs whom I respected, several of whom had told me privately that Paterson was 'guilty as charged', including Robert Buckland, the former justice secretary, who had previously sat on the Standards Committee, signed the amendment, as did six MPs who had had an adverse finding against them from the commissioner in the last year.

A lot was at stake. For Paterson, a thirty-day suspension would invoke the Recall of MPs Act of 2015. This stipulates that, if an MP is suspended for ten sitting days or more following the recommendation of the Standards Committee, they can face a special by-election if 10 per cent of their constituents attend one of ten specially appointed offices to sign a petition calling for it within six weeks. Paterson had a very safe seat, with a majority of 22,949, and many MPs therefore thought that if he took his medicine and sought forgiveness, his constituents would let him carry on. But there was always the risk that he would be humiliated. More importantly, he wasn't the kind of MP who takes kindly to being told off.

There was even more at stake for the Commons as a whole. The House had never, so far as I could see after a lengthy trawl of the history books, voted down a recommendation from the Standards Committee or its predecessor, the Standards and Privileges Committee.* The only instance where it had even amended a recommendation was when it increased the sanction, as it did in 1947, when it expelled the Labour MP Garry Allighan for an 'aggravated contempt and gross breach of privilege' (namely, claiming that MPs gave journalists private information about parliamentary meetings in exchange for cash or drinks, when in actual fact he himself had sold information to the *Evening Standard*) rather than suspend him for six months as the Committee had recommended.[3] In the autumn of 2021 it felt as if the Johnson government was summarily dispensing with due process. MPs on all sides feared that that would lower us even further in the eyes of the public, and many of the longer-standing members despaired that we were returning to the follies of the parliamentary expenses scandal of 2008/9, when five MPs and two peers went to prison for false claims and many more had to repay

---

*The Committee of Privileges, which had existed since the sixteenth century, became the Standards and Privileges Committee in 1995, when the post of parliamentary commissioner for standards was created. The Committee was split in two in 2013, when lay members were added to the committee. Seven MPs now form the Committee of Privileges and join the seven lay members to form the Committee on Standards. The lay members have no political allegiance and can never have been an MP or a peer. The Committee adjudicates on breaches of the Code of Conduct. A parallel body, the Independent Expert Panel, adjudicates on cases of bullying, harassment and sexual misconduct – and hears appeals against decisions of the Standards Committee.

money and left parliament. All of us, though, were of course aware that the universally popular Conservative MP Sir David Amess had been brutally murdered less than three weeks previously. At that time we had united in grief across the party divide. Now the government was dragging parliament into the mud. As one Tory MP texted me, 'There have been times when I have been ashamed of being a Member of this House, I don't want to go back to that.'

The debate on 3 November was a mess, politically, procedurally and emotionally. It was also nasty, brutish and short – just ninety minutes long. The bruising, partisan nature of the proceedings had been set by Prime Minister's Questions (PMQs), when Angela Rayner (standing in for the leader of the Opposition Sir Keir Starmer, who was self-isolating with Covid) accused Johnson of operating 'one rule for Conservative Members and another rule for the rest of us', and Johnson breezily made it clear he was supporting Leadsom's amendment.[4] This truly shocked me. I wrote in my diary, 'Johnson seems to think that he can do anything, however dodgy, mendacious or incompetent, and still be loved.' After a statement on the climate conference COP26 (which was given only so as to buy time for the government to rally its troops), Rees-Mogg started the debate at 2.01 p.m. The leader of the House is meant to try to carry the whole House, but that would require him to be emollient and to eschew pomposity. Instead, he was patronising, partisan and disingenuous. He said it was his role 'as Leader of the House to listen to the concerns and thoughts of Members *on both sides of the House*, which are now too numerous to ignore'.[5] But he knew perfectly well that it was only a handful of Tory MPs who were unhappy with the Committee report. He said he did not come 'to defend my right hon. Friend the Member for North Shropshire', but that was precisely what he did, repeating word for word the arguments Paterson had made in the media. He invoked the pompous Latin legal tag, 'Let justice be done though the heavens fall', to suggest that this was one of the greatest ever miscarriages of justice; and he quoted Portia's speech from *The Merchant of Venice*: 'The quality of mercy is not strained.' It was stomach-turning, sententious guff and, despite saying he would take thirty minutes, he took forty-four, nearly half the total he had allowed for the debate. A senior Brexiteer Tory MP told me later in the gym, 'I don't think he believed a word of what he said.' I sat there fuming but determined to keep calm. I knew our argument was strong because it was based on a fair and rigorous examination of the facts.

It got worse when Leadsom spoke. She had been told the Opposition would support her amendment, but Labour, the SNP and the Liberal Democrats made it abundantly clear that they would not participate in the proposed committee. John Whittingdale said he had not been asked whether he wanted to chair it – and rang me to say it was all madness. In a complete breach with tradition, which stipulates that a member should leave the chamber when their conduct is being debated, Paterson sat there with a face like thunder throughout. Emotions ran high. The Father and the Mother of the House, Sir Peter Bottomley and Harriet Harman, made it clear they thought the amendment was misguided. William Cash made an incomprehensible speech suggesting it was all a travesty of justice – and then it was over to me, as the Speaker had decided I should speak last.

One of the Tory MPs on the committee, Mark Fletcher, had helpfully advised me the night before that

I should be measured. 'After all,' he said, 'you tend to be 80 per cent brilliant and 20 per cent crap.' I started by addressing Paterson directly and acknowledging the horrible circumstances of Rose Paterson's death. 'I wish to express my sincere condolences to him,' I said. 'I have known suicide in my family, as he knows, and [when I was a curate I] performed many funerals for suicides. I know the grief, the anguish, and often the guilt that is associated. The last year must have been very distressing for him, and the Committee took those circumstances fully into account when considering his conduct.' That, however, did not change the fundamental point. Nor did it excuse the amendment. 'It is the very definition of injustice that one should change the rules or the process at the very last moment, and do so for a named individual. That is what the amendment does. Retrospective legislation to favour or damage an individual because they are a friend or a foe is immoral and the polar opposite of the rule of law.'[6] I ended with a warning to the House, 'do not do something today that we will rue in the future'. I had tried to be straight, calm and quiet – but was probably rather pompous. A few Tories texted to say I had changed their vote and they would no longer support the amendment.

The vote came immediately after I sat down. It's a physical thing, voting in the Commons. It involves deciding which lobby to walk through, or whether to sit on your hands and not vote at all. It makes it very easy to spot people who are not normally in the same lobby as you. We took the amendment first, for which I and my colleagues were in the No lobby. None of the Tory members of the Committee were with us (they abstained), so I presumed the government would have an easy win, especially as the government whips were doing their best imitation of vultures, hovering round the tearoom and lurking outside the toilets. But I knew a few others, including most of the Tories on the Foreign Affairs Select Committee with me, had decided to absent themselves (Royston Smith told me he was washing his hair – he is bald). However, I could see several braver Tories in the lobby with us and started counting Aaron Bell, Jackie Doyle-Price, Richard Fuller, Kate Griffiths, Mark Harper (another former chief whip), Simon Hoare, Kevin Hollinrake, Nigel Mills, Jill Mortimer, Holly Mumby-Croft, Matthew Offord, John Stevenson and William Wragg. I still wasn't optimistic. The government had a majority of eighty, so thirteen rebels wouldn't be enough. We gathered back in the chamber and were joined by the four tellers – two from the government for those in favour of the amendment and two from the Opposition for those against – who count members through the lobbies and verify the tally. The government tellers for the Ayes, Scott Mann and Michael Tomlinson, stood on the side that announces the result, so we all knew they had won. It was closer than I had thought: 250 ayes to 232 noes (52 per cent to 48). The amendment was carried by eighteen votes. Johnson had saved his man. And at 3.57 p.m. we moved on to the Nuclear Energy (Financing) Bill.

Owen Paterson then began claiming on every television and radio channel that would have him that he had been completely vindicated. Lots of Tories had been in touch immediately after the vote to say it was all a terrible mistake, but I felt we (and I) had failed miserably. We had hit rock bottom. The House had knowingly endorsed an 'egregious case of paid advocacy',[7] i.e. a serious breach of the rules, and the fact that every Tory who voted for the amendment would be tarred with that brush was little consolation. Depressed and angry, I was on my way to dinner with my husband – and that took me through Westminster Hall.

The Hall is peaceful and stunning, especially when it is empty, late at night or early in the morning. Its eleventh-century stone walls look as solidly permanent as any edifice could be, its expansive fourteenth-century hammerbeam oak roof seems to rest gently on the wings of twenty-six carved angels, and its vast flagstones look worn down by the boots, shoes, stilettos, mules, plimsolls and trainers of more than forty generations of monarchs, MPs, peers and members of the public. The Hall is best known for hosting the lying-in-state of every monarch since Edward VII. But for many centuries it had a very different state purpose. This was where state trials for treason were held. Here William Wallace was tried in 1305, seated on a bench at the south end wearing an ironic crown of laurels. Afterwards horses dragged him through London to Smithfield where he was stripped naked before being hanged, drawn and quartered. A brass plaque in the floor also commemorates the trial in 1535 of Thomas More (Sir Thomas or St Thomas depending on your point of view), during which he was allowed no lawyer and was given no idea of the charges against him. He too was sentenced to death, although the King allowed him a less brutal, swifter execution by beheading. There were many more such trials. Guy Fawkes and his co-conspirators, the earls of Essex and of Strafford, the Jacobite rebels and the former governor-general of Bengal, Warren Hastings, all faced juries there. It was rarely a fair trial, as the court was rigged, the charges were trumped up and the evidence was made up. It felt less like a court of justice than a marketplace, too, as MPs wandered around eating, drinking, chatting and enjoying the spectacle. Other courts had sat in the Hall down the years, but this was where the state put its most famous miscreants on trial for treason. And then executed them.

As I stood there on 3 November, I felt the tables had turned, as parliament itself was now on trial. I thought the case against Paterson was clear. As I had told any colleagues who had had their arms twisted by the whips and wondered what to do in the run-up to the vote, 'Just read the Standards Committee report.' Many who did had abstained or voted with us. But for the first time in its history the House had voted down a recommendation of the Standards Committee. That implied we no longer cared about standards. I know some voters think we never did, but I felt this was a dangerous moment.

The government position didn't last. Kwasi Kwarteng ludicrously called for Kathryn Stone to consider resigning as commissioner and Sir Christopher Chope kept on defending the indefensible, but Paterson's media round so sickened everyone else that even ministers and his close friends abandoned him the next day. In one of the most abject instances of a feigned apology and with about as much grace as a flatulent hippopotamus, Rees-Mogg told the House, 'I fear last night's debate conflated the individual case with the general concern.'[8] This had been as plain as a pikestaff the moment the amendment was tabled – and there was no 'general concern' – but this was Rees-Mogg's slippery way of admitting that the amendment he had so passionately supported less than twenty-four hours previously was an unmitigated mistake. His volte-face did the trick, though. With the writing on the wall now burning in letters several storeys high, Paterson announced the following day that he was standing down, and angrily claimed that he had been betrayed. On 16 November, less than two weeks after the original vote, Rees-Mogg reluctantly ate another slice of not very humble pie and the House finally and unanimously endorsed the Standards Committee report. This time Rees-Mogg even had the cheek to say with a straight face, 'Paid lobbying is wrong and Members found guilty of it should pay the necessary penalties.'[9] Speaking after him, Johnson's predecessor as prime minister, Theresa May (who had been at COP26 on the day of the vote) summed up the government's behaviour in a stinging attack. 'The attempt by right honourable and honourable Members of this House,' she said, 'aided and abetted by the Government under cover of reform of the process, effectively to clear [Paterson's] name was misplaced, ill-judged and just plain wrong.'[10] Yes, quite, I thought.

History has nicknamed parliaments down the years. There was the Mad Parliament, the Model Parliament, the Unlearned Parliament (which banned lawyers), the Long, the Short and the Rump Parliaments. The Good Parliament of 1375 courageously tackled fraud and corruption in the court of Edward III but was followed a year later by the Bad Parliament, which corruptly undid all its predecessor's work and introduced an unpopular poll tax, leading to the Peasants' Revolt. (The two parliaments also sat so long that they wore out the floor covering in the octagonal Chapter House of Westminster Abbey.) In a similar vein, the Oxford historian Professor Jonathan Healey reckons the Merciless Parliament of 1388 (which followed the Wonderful Parliament of 1386) might have been created 'by forcing a nest of wasps to mate with Katie Hopkins, and cramming their multiple spawn together into a poorly ventilated Wetherspoons toilet'.[11] It convicted several of Richard II's closest companions, without trial, of 'living in vice, deluding the said king [and] embracing the mammon of iniquity for themselves' and ordered the execution of dozens of the king's allies and servants. Modern parallels with medieval parliament are invidious, but the MPs who were summoned to Leicester Castle in 1426 so hated each other that when swords were banned they brought the medieval equivalent of baseball bats, hence it being named the Parliament of Bats, which rather puts the rowdiness of modern Prime Minister's Questions in the shade. Yet the years of parliamentary shenanigans since 2010 have seen similar epithets applied. Angela Eagle was so frustrated by the coalition government's lack of action that she called the 2010–15 parliament 'the Zombie parliament', and Jacob Rees-Mogg, recalling the Addled Parliament of 1614, which refused to do James VI and I's bidding, told the Commons that the 2017–19 Parliament 'is indeed an addled Parliament that is not able to get things done'.[12] Others suggested that because of its failure to implement Brexit, it should be known as the Turncoat, the Traitor, the Quisling or the Remoaners' Parliament.

But how should we describe this parliament? Is it another 'Bad Parliament', the 'Parliament of Shenanigans', the 'Pinocchio Parliament' or the 'Parliament of Crooks'? The artist Chris Orr RA has called it 'the parliament of the long noses' because of the endless lies, and one colleague calls it the 'Rump' (as in backside). But maybe, if we can get our act together and put sensible measures in place in short order, it could be the 'Fixed Parliament' (as in mended). It may be that such reform will have to await a change of government, but it will never happen unless we build the will to change. Which is what this book is about – why we need to fix parliament and how we can do it.

However, before we get down to brass tacks, I want to issue a couple of public health warnings about what you are about to read.

First of all, please put this book back on the shelf if you are expecting an endless excoriating attack on all MPs as wasters, losers, bullies, perverts, liars and crooks. I wouldn't describe all my worst political opponents like that. When criticising Matt Hancock's decision to travel to the Australian jungle to participate in the 2022 series of *I'm a Celebrity … Get Me Out of Here!*, Rishi Sunak said, 'I think politics at its best can and should be actually quite noble.'[13] I agree. Every MP I know went into politics for noble reasons. They want to change the world for the better. When I look around the Commons, I see dozens of people who have made a lasting difference for good. Week after week, Diana Johnson (now Dame Diana) called for an independent inquiry into the infected blood scandal and, thanks to her, families are finally getting the compensation they deserved. When Dame Cheryl Gillan died in 2021, she was remembered more for her successful campaign for a national strategy for autism than for her two years in the Cabinet as secretary of state for Wales. Dame Andrea Leadsom has done invaluable work on early years to help every baby get the best start in life. And it's not just the dames. Stella Creasey on payday loans, Carolyn Harris on the menopause, Tracey Crouch on football, Johnny Mercer on veterans' issues, Liam Fox on Down's Syndrome, Pauline Latham on skin cancer – I could go on. We are as varied as the trees in the forest. Some good, some bad, some mostly good and partly bad. Their version of changing the world may differ. Some of their political ideas may to my mind be completely round the twist, unfeeling or cruel, but that doesn't mean their original motivation was misguided, let alone evil.

Yes, it's also true that power – even the limited power enjoyed by a backbench MP – can poison the soul. As I know from my own bitter experience of skin cancer, we get burnt if we sit too long in the sun; and too long a spell in high office can dull our self-awareness and sharpen our sense of entitlement. That's when a weak minister transforms into a hectoring bully. And it's also true, as Sunak put it, in what many interpreted as another sideswipe at Hancock, that it was 'incumbent on all members of parliament to do the things that earn people's respect'.[14] It may surprise you to know that MPs do normally rise to the occasion. Just think of Sir Charles Walker's extraordinarily candid speech about living with OCD in 2012 – which was perfectly mirrored by his Labour opponent, Kevan Jones, who spoke of his struggle with depression. Or take the moment when the kindly DUP MP Jim Shannon was talking about his Christian faith in the last debate of the year in 2022. He had just said, 'I thank my long-suffering wife, who is definitely long-suffering,' and then mentioned his 91-year-old mum. Suddenly tears flowed and he couldn't carry on. The House was transfixed as we all willed him to find his composure, but the leader of the House, Penny Mordaunt, intervened on him solely to allow him a moment to calm back down. She warbled about absolutely nothing for a minute – and when he got back on his feet he was fine. Some accuse MPs of looking after one another like a self-interested cabal, but there are moments when our shared humanity shines through.[15]

Besides, the seven principles of public life which were drawn up in 1995 by the Committee on Standards in Public Life under its first chairman, Lord Nolan – selflessness, integrity, objectivity, accountability, openness, honesty and leadership (the 'Nolan Principles') – are an important guiding compass in public life, but they are aspirations not rules. They have to be interpreted by each one of us. Selflessness, for instance, if taken at the extreme, could mean that every MP should work for nothing, abjure a private or a family life and survive on a diet of husks and offcuts. Also, by that definition, no MP should be ambitious. Yet putting yourself forward for election requires a degree of self-belief and the drag queen RuPaul has a point when she says, 'If you can't love yourself, how in the hell you gonna love someone else?'

Hang on, hang on, I hear you say, surely we should expect better of our political leaders? Yes, I agree. Public life comes with public expectations. That is what this book is all about. And yes, we have got ourselves in a mess in recent years. Yet if we rant and rave about all MPs, as if they are all equally dire, we merely subvert democracy itself. The manifest failings of many of today's politicians may tempt us to bring down the whole edifice, like Samson in the temple, but that way madness lies. Moreover, it infuriates me when people pretend all sins are equally bad or make an equivalence between minor and major misdemeanours. Registering £300 of free hospitality after the twenty-eight-day deadline is one thing, paid advocacy on behalf of a client another.

I should also say that, although I am a Labour MP and will do everything I can to secure a Labour government, this book is not a partisan polemic. No political party is an unadulterated congregation of saints, and historically the Labour Party has had its fair share of miscreants. Just think of John Stonehouse or Keith Vaz. Inevitably, government gets the lion's share of my complaints about the system, but I would be making the same comments whoever was in power. Moreover, I am writing in my personal capacity, not as the chair of the Standards Committee. In any case that post, which according to the standing orders of the Commons has to be held by an Opposition MP, is elected by the whole House and is not a partisan post. The Committee tries to proceed by consensus even if that means a very long meeting to agree a report – and that in turn requires that I act impartially. I hope this book embodies that same principle.

This takes me to my second health warning about this book. I am not a saint, so please put it down if you thought I was, because I don't want you to be sorely disappointed. I have got into more political scrapes than most and every one of my friends – and most of my opponents – will tell you how naughty/infuriating/despicable I can be. I'm not going to list the many mistakes and misdemeanours of my more than two decades in parliament – you can look it up online if you want, as several newspapers have obliged over the years – but perhaps the decent thing about me is that I know my failings better than anyone. I can be impulsive, sanctimonious and pompous. Sir Christopher Chope (him again) recently said of me, 'he thinks very highly of himself'[16] – and he probably has a point. I like the sound of my own voice and sometimes I crack an inappropriate joke at the wrong moment. I've been known to leap into action without seeing the full picture and I have dark agonies of guilt pretty much every month. When I am cross I am very cross. I know there are occasions when

I have got my facts wrong, and the whirligig of politics has spun so fast I haven't corrected the record. I have often said I find it ironic that I chair of the House of Commons Committee on Standards. Others think my failings make me a hypocrite. They say I don't practise what I preach. But, partly because I hate being judged for my sexuality, I'm not a very judgemental person. I try to respect my opponents and my detractors, even when that is difficult, because I was taught the Golden Rule, 'Do unto others as you would have done unto you.' Tolerance is a decent principle, but respect is harder and better. So, perhaps because of my failings, I am more realistic than other self-appointed arbiters when it comes to standards in public life. I don't expect perfection. On occasion my understanding of the proper compromises involved in politics may infuriate you.

So, why should I write this book? My central qualification is that I have probably studied the history of parliament more than any other MP and I am a bit of a rules freak. I haven't just read Erskine May, the principle guide to parliamentary protocol, I have read several different editions of it – and occasionally exchange notes with the clerk of the House about elements that need updating.[17] I love asking the Speaker to rule on a point of order about the proper conduct of business. I have written extensively about the constitution. For two years I worked in the office of the leader of the House, as PPS (parliamentary private secretary) and then deputy leader. And in 2020 I became chair of the Standards and Privileges Committees, just when we started considering drafting a new Code of Conduct.

In this book, we will be covering every aspect of parliamentary conduct. Chapter 1 asks whether this is the worst parliament in history in terms of the conduct of MPs. I move on to look at parliament's wider systemic and structural problems, which largely centre round our 'winner takes all' constitution (Chapter 2), and the capricious and corrupt way ministers use and abuse their powers (Chapter 3). I then consider three specific failings on the part of individual MPs: lies, liars and lying (Chapter 4); bullying, harassment and sexual misconduct (Chapter 5); and second jobs and other conflicts of interest (Chapter 6). Finally, I include suggestions for how we could help ourselves and fix some of these problems (Chapter 7).

Which brings me to a final point before we start. MPs aspire to very high ideals. The prayers before the start of formal business never vary. Every day, we turn to face the wall (for some completely unknown reason) while the chaplain prays that we 'may never lead the nation wrongly through love of power, desire to please or unworthy ideals, but laying aside all private interests and prejudices keep in mind [our] responsibility to seek to improve the condition of all mankind'. Could there be more evidence of our 'desire to please' than the fact that every week the government and the major parties commission polling among key segments of the voting public to work out what policies are popular and might win an election? Could any one of us truly put their hand on their heart and say they have no 'love of power'? And do we always lay aside 'all private interests and prejudices'? Of course not. If we did, there would be no political parties, and none of us would aspire to high office. But here I want to issue a corrective. My boss when I was a curate in High Wycombe was the Reverend Michael Roberts, a sage, generous and liberal man with a warm heart, who went on to lead the theological college Westcott House. I turned to him for advice when I was preparing my first couple for marriage (which I realise was presumptuous, considering I was gay, single and terrified of commitment). He said the main thing was to give the couple a chance to be open with each other about things they might never have said to each other anywhere else, including household finances and how to deal with anger. 'What do I say about being a parent?' I asked. 'Look,' he said, 'there is no point loading parents up with guilt by trying to get them to be perfect parents, or even good parents. It's far better to help them aspire to be *good enough* parents. They might actually manage that.' That's my feeling about MPs, too. As it is, most of us crucify ourselves with guilt about not doing enough for others. I work hard, but I don't claim to be a good MP, and I don't seek to lecture my colleagues on how to be good. I'd just like us to be good enough.

1

The Worst Parliament in History?

It was a propitious day, Monday, the seventeenth day of the second month of 1727, and a crowd had gathered outside Westminster Hall, including many MPs and lords. Other venues for the pillory were more commonly used, but the man in the stocks that day was John Ward, the former MP for the corrupt borough seat of Weymouth and Melcombe Regis. Ward had a keen eye for a commercial opportunity and very sharp elbows, thanks to which he had risen from rags to riches and amassed a fortune. But in the process he had spent £6,000 on bribing voters, defrauded the duke of Buckingham of £70,000, he had badgered the dowager duchess and threatened her staff, salted away money from his creditors, been expelled from the Commons and absconded for eight months. When he was tracked down, he was convicted of forgery, fined £500 and sentenced to a spell in the pillory. A strong body of constables was meant to protect him from the baying mob, but by the time he was taken down he was senseless and bleeding at the mouth, having been repeatedly pelted with whatever came to hand, including eggs, ordure and dead cats.

The pillory was rightly abolished in 1837, but if you were to read the opinion polls you would conclude that the court of public opinion (which is in permanent session) would happily send at least half of the present parliament to the stocks if it could. I understand the feeling. When I became chair of the Standards Committee in the spring of 2020, I was told it would be a quiet gig, with little to do and even less to catch the public attention. Diligent housekeeping was all that was required. Boy, was that wrong. Every week seems to have brought a new parliamentary scandal, varying from the trivial to the career-defining, and just when things seem to be calming down, something new comes along. For a while I thought that once Johnson and his hapless successor as PM Liz Truss had handed back the seals of office, the ship of state would right itself. But, within moments of arriving in Downing Street, Rishi Sunak faced calls to sack Suella Braverman, Sir Gavin Williamson, Dominic Raab and Nadhim Zahawi and the scandals have not let up since.

The truth is, politicians have rarely been seen in quite such a negative light as they are today. The opinion polling is stark. Gallup found in 1944 that just over a third of voters thought politicians were 'out for themselves'. That figure stood at 48 per cent in 2014, but polling done by YouGov in May 2021 suggested it was by then 57 per cent, and when they repeated it in December 2021 it stood at 63 per cent. Another poll for the Constitution Unit at University College London (UCL) found that, of those who expressed a view, 52 per cent thought politicians followed a lower ethical standard than most ordinary citizens – and only 4 per cent thought they followed a higher standard. Several things can make these figures fluctuate – the Greensill and Partygate scandals (over David Cameron's lobbying of government ministers on behalf of the financial services company Greensill, and the illegal parties at Downing Street during lockdown) had an obvious effect in 2021 and people who lived furthest from Westminster tended to distrust it most – but when nearly two-thirds of voters think that badly of their elected representatives, democracy is in trouble.

Others roll their eyes at such talk and shout, 'Do calm down, dear. Don't exaggerate. Stop showboating.' I'm endlessly being told, for instance, that Owen Paterson was just 'one bad apple'. But the very phrase 'one bad apple' exposes the dangerous complacency I'm talking about. After all, the whole point is not that the one bad apple is an exception but that it spoils the rest of the barrel, as blight spreads. People knew this as long ago as the fourteenth century when Geoffrey Chaucer's trainee chef Perkin says in 'The Cook's Tale' that it is better to take the one rotten apple out of the hoard than let it rot the rest, or, for that matter, sack one bad servant before he ruins all the others.* You could say that's what we (eventually) did with Paterson. Parliament – and public clamour – made him walk. But the problem is that 250 MPs seemingly saw nothing wrong in what he had done and voted to defend him. As I said, blight spreads.

THE FACTS OF THE CASE

But is this the worst parliament in history? Is that fair? How bad a state are we in?

The charge sheet is long – and damning. At the time of writing, twenty-two MPs have either been suspended by the House, resigned their seats or left the chamber before

---

*Geoffrey would have known something about bad apples. He was a member of the Wonderful Parliament in 1386, but missed the Merciless Parliament two years later (which turfed out corrupt officials). His son Thomas was elected Speaker five times.

being suspended for a day or more since the general election in December 2019. That is statistically the worst record of any parliament in our history, by a long chalk. The offences have varied. Conor Burns (Conservative) was suspended for seven days for using parliamentary privilege* to threaten someone on behalf of his father. He resigned as a minister but was later reinstated. Rob Roberts (Conservative) was suspended for six weeks for sexually inappropriate behaviour with a member of staff. Thanks to a loophole in the law, which has now been closed, he was not subject to the Recall of MPs Act and remains an MP. Five Conservative MPs attempted to circumvent a trial judge to keep secret character witness statements made in support of Charlie Elphicke MP, who had been convicted on three counts of sexual assault. Two of them (Adam Holloway and Bob Stewart) were told to apologise formally to the House and three (Theresa Villiers, Sir Roger Gale and Natalie Elphicke) were suspended from the House for a single day, but so nonchalant was the government about their behaviour that one of those who was suspended, Elphicke's wife and successor as MP for Dover, Natalie Elphicke, was allowed to remain as a PPS. The Independent Expert Panel (IEP) which adjudicates on cases of bullying, harassment and sexual misconduct, required Daniel Kawczynski (Conservative) to apologise to the House for bullying a member of parliamentary staff, but when he undermined that apology by telling a radio station he had only done so to avoid being suspended, the IEP complained to the Standards Committee, which

---

*Parliamentary privilege grants MPs and peers certain legal immunities, including immunity from prosecution for anything they say in a parliamentary proceeding. It is essential to MPs' freedom of speech.

recommended he be suspended for a day. The Labour MP Liam Byrne and the Scottish National Party's Patrick Grady were suspended for two days, Byrne for bullying and Grady for making sexual advances to a member of staff. Andrew Bridgen (Conservative) appealed against the Standards Committee recommendation that he be suspended for five days for paid advocacy and attempting to bully the parliamentary commissioner, but the appeal body (the IEP) decided that his letter to the commissioner was 'a calculated piece of spite' and that the sanction 'could properly and fairly have been more severe'.[1] Neil Coyle (Labour) was suspended for five sitting days for inappropriate and racist remarks made to a journalist in the Strangers' Bar. Margaret Ferrier (SNP) was suspended for thirty days for bringing the House into disrepute by breaching Covid rules recklessly and culpably.

Some have jumped before they were pushed. Mike Hill (Labour) resigned prior to an adverse finding of the IEP, Imran Ahmad Khan (Conservative) resigned after being convicted of sexual assault of a minor but before his (unsuccessful) appeal was heard, Neil Parish (Conservative) – accused of watching pornography on his mobile phone in the chamber – resigned before an investigation was launched, Christian Matheson (Labour) resigned when the IEP recommended he be suspended for sexually inappropriate behaviour with one of his staff. In addition, Drew Hendry (SNP), Kenny MacAskill (Alba) and Neale Hanvey (Alba) were named by the Speaker and excluded for five days each for refusing to accept the authority of the chair, and Dawn Butler (Labour) and Ian Blackford (SNP) were forced to retire from the House for a day when they refused to withdraw an accusation that the prime minister had lied.

MPs sanctioned in the 2019 parliament

Date	Name	Offence
11 May 2020	Conor Burns (Con)	Abuse of privilege
16 Dec 2020	Drew Hendry (SNP)	Disorderly conduct
16 Mar 2021	Mike Hill (Lab)	Sexual harassment
27 May 2021	Rob Roberts (Con)	Sexual harassment
22 Jul 2021	Dawn Butler (Lab)	Disorderly conduct
9 Sept 2021	Theresa Villiers (Con)	Interfering in a judicial proceeding
9 Sept 2021	Sir Roger Gale (Con)	Interfering in a judicial proceeding
9 Sept 2021	Natalie Elphicke (Con)	Interfering in a judicial proceeding
5 Nov 2021	Owen Paterson (Con)	Paid lobbying
20 Jan 2022	Daniel Kawczynski (Con)	Undermining his apology
31 Jan 2022	Ian Blackford (SNP)	Disorderly conduct
3 May 2022	Imran Khan (Con)	Sexual assault of a minor
4 May 2022	Neil Parish (Con)	Watching porn
11 May 2022	Liam Byrne (Lab)	Bullying
15 Jun 2022	Patrick Grady (SNP)	Sexual harassment
13 Jul 2022	Kenny MacAskill (Alba)	Disorderly conduct
13 Jul 2022	Neale Hanvey (Alba)	Disorderly conduct
21 Oct 2022	Christian Matheson (Lab)	Sexual misconduct
3 Nov 2022	Andrew Bridgen (Con)	Paid lobbying and bullying the Commissioner
3 Mar 2023	Neil Coyle (Lab)	Abuse and harassment
30 Mar 2023	Margaret Ferrier (SNP)	Bringing the House into disrepute
9 June 2023	Boris Johnson (Con)	Misleading the House

Sanctioning body	Result
Standards	Seven days' suspension
Speaker	Five days' suspension
IEP	Resigned before report
IEP	Six weeks' suspension
Speaker	One day's suspension
Standards	Apology and one day's suspension
Standards	Apology and one day's suspension
Standards	Apology and one day's suspension
Standards	Resigned before thirty-day suspension agreed
Standards	One day's suspension
Speaker	One day's suspension
Crown Court	Resigned
n/a	Resigned
IEP	Two days' suspension
IEP	Two days' suspension
Speaker	Five days' suspension
Speaker	Five days' suspension
IEP	Resigned before four-week suspension
Standards and IEP on appeal	Five days' suspension
IEP	Five days' suspension
Standards and IEP on appeal	Thirty days' suspension
Privileges	Resigned before publication of report

That is not all. Three MPs have been required to apologise to the House by the Standards Committee, and the group of 'independent' MPs (i.e. those who have been suspended by their respective parties pending misconduct investigations, often for unspecified allegations) has at times been larger than the Liberal Democrat group (and includes the former Labour chief whip, Nick Brown, the former Tory deputy chief whip, Chris Pincher and Matt Hancock). One unnamed Conservative MP has also been told not to attend the parliamentary estate as the police are investigating him for a series of serious offences, and according to the *Sun*, 'a SENIOR Conservative MP has been reported to police over allegations of rape and an alleged string of sexual assaults.'[2] Three recent MPs have also been convicted of serious crimes – Jared O'Mara, Paul Clark and Charlie Elphicke. Of course, MPs sometimes infuriate their constituents through the policies they adopt or the way they vote, but that is a matter for the ballot box. And even matters that would never lead to a prosecution or standards investigation can understandably wind the public up, like when an MP gives the finger to the crowd outside Downing Street; or when it is revealed that a minister got a Covid test specially couriered for a colleague's child; or when that same minister takes a hefty fee to jet off to Australia to appear on a reality TV show when parliament is sitting; or when a former prime minister engages in repeated lobbying of his erstwhile colleagues on behalf of a finance company (which later collapsed) in which he had shares that netted him £3.3 million; or when former ministers are caught in a sting operation offering their services at £10,000 a day; or when a backbench MP is caught in another sting offering to provide a leaked copy of a government white paper in advance of publication.

Worst of all is the sense that there is one rule for them and another for the rest of us.

Ministers have added to the sense of ethical collapse. Leaving aside those who left office voluntarily over political differences (such as Brexit), the following have been forced out of ministerial office for some kind of misdemeanour or other since 2017: Sir Michael Fallon over allegations of inappropriate sexual behaviour; Chris Pincher over allegations of sexual harassment; Priti Patel over secret meetings with the Israeli government; Damian Green over misleading statements about images on his office computer; Andrew Griffiths over allegations of sexual misconduct; Alun Cairns following claims that he had known about a former aide's role in undermining a rape trial; Gavin Williamson for leaking highly classified information; Matt Hancock for breaching his own social distancing rules when he was health secretary; Chris Pincher (again) over reports that he had drunkenly groped two men at the Carlton Club; Suella Braverman for breaching the Ministerial Code on multiple occasions; Gavin Williamson (again) over bullying texts sent to another minister; Nadhim Zahawi over his failure to disclose a substantial HMRC penalty; and Dominic Raab for bullying. To top it all, sixty-two ministers, PPSs and other government appointees resigned in a single day to force Boris Johnson out of office for a catalogue of errors, misdemeanours and deceptions. In all, 147 ministers and aides left the government in 2022.

The kernel of this hard nut has been a widespread sense that politicians believe the rules don't apply to them. Covid was part of it. Thousands of people have a private story of how they abided by the Covid rules despite terrible personal anguish. Lonely deaths. Empty funerals. Hands not held. Weddings postponed. Long, painful isolation. But Matt Hancock (and the PM's chief adviser Dominic Cummings) broke the rules and made up facile excuses; and Downing Street partied – and lied about it. The entitled air of those at the top infuriated not just the nation but many MPs, including Tories. And when other stories surfaced, about personal protective equipment (PPE) contracts for friends and about who knew what when about Chris Pincher, more lies were told, giving the impression that you could get away with anything if you had a friend in high places.

Some think this is the usual kerfuffle of parliamentary politics – the normal ups and downs, ins and outs. But the chaos it has produced in the daily business of government has been completely out of the ordinary, and immensely harmful to the UK. Just imagine what it is like as a backbench MP (of whichever hue) trying to sort out a non-partisan constituency issue. I'll give one example from my own constituency. An old railway tunnel connects the village of Blaencwm at the top of the Rhondda Fawr to Blaengwynfi in the Afan Valley. It has been closed for years, but there are plans to reopen it and transform it into the second-longest cycle tunnel in Europe. It would be a great tourist attraction in a beautiful but deprived part of the South Wales Valleys. For some strange reason, despite being in Wales, it belongs to the UK Department of Transport, so for the last three years I have been trying to get government ministers on board (forgive the pun). First, I met the secretary of state, Grant Shapps. He was very enthusiastic and charged his junior minister Chris Heaton-Harris with looking into it. Two days later Heaton-Harris was moved to another department as Europe minister – and he later became chief whip and then the Northern Ireland secretary. In the meantime, I tried to get a meeting with his replacement, Wendy Morton, but unfortunately she then became the chief whip, she resigned, she unresigned and then she was sacked when Liz Truss fell. As for Shapps, he too was sacked and then became the home secretary and then secretary of state for business, energy and industrial strategy before having his department reorganised as the Department for Energy Security and Net Zero. I was going to meet with his short-lived replacement, Anne-Marie Trevelyan, but she was swiftly moved to the Foreign, Commonwealth and Development Office. Since then, I have spoken to the latest secretary of state, Mark Harper, but he passed me on to the minister of state, Huw Merriman, who has passed me on to the parliamentary under-secretary, Richard Holdern. So far there has been no resolution. We haven't – so far – even managed to get all the right people round the table at the same time. I tell this tale solely to point out that the ministerial whirligig has consequences. I'm just an MP talking about a single tourism project in my constituency. Imagine if I were a senior figure in a nationally significant industry. Or the governor of the Bank of England dealing with four chancellors of the Exchequer in a year.

ARGY-BARGY IN THE CHAMBER

Voters have another longstanding but equally potent gripe which has combined with their anger about the misconduct rife in the 2019 parliament in a particularly toxic way. The rule (from 1693) that no member should 'presume to make any Noise or Disturbance, whilst any Member shall be orderly debating' is systematically and noisily ignored on a daily basis (or, as Hamlet put it, is 'more honoured in the breach than the observance'), and the consequent argy-bargy across the chamber is often childish, boorish, intimidating and completely counter-productive, especially at Prime Minister's Questions.[3] Some politicians blame the rowdiness on the shape of the chamber, which was modelled on the original home of the Commons, the medieval Chapel of St Stephen's, which had benches facing each other. It means that the government and Opposition confront one another physically. You are, by definition, on one side or the other. But there's no excuse for sane adult MPs turning into toddlers, screaming, bellowing, howling with fake laughter and (worst of all) deliberately sledging their opponents (with encouragement from the whips). Voters hate this. A poll by Opinium for Compassion in Politics published in June 2022 showed that 43 per cent of voters said watching parliamentary debates made them respect MPs less, compared to 5 per cent who said it increased their respect for us. It is difficult not to agree with Jennifer Nadel, the co-director of Compassion in Politics, who has said, 'A basic rule of thumb is: if you are not allowed to do it in a classroom or a place of work you most certainly should not be allowed to do it in Parliament no matter how many years of tradition have allowed it to continue.'[4]

However, there are some strengths to this way of doing things. One of them is that the despatch box at which ministers stand (and on which they rest their notes, their elbows or their bellies) is the embodiment of ministerial accountability. No prime minister can evade the House for long. Whatever you think of the decision to invade Iraq, Tony Blair had to come to the Commons to defend his decision, whereas George Bush never even had to address a press conference, let alone face a roomful of hard-nosed critics and political opponents. Spontaneity is often the only way we get to the unvarnished truth, as a minister caught off-guard by an unexpected or witty question may divulge far more than they intended. We need to reform PMQs so that the most senior figure in the land is properly put on the spot rather than subjected to a pantomime, but we mustn't throw the baby out with the bathwater. We should have proper questions – and answers. The Speaker should stop the sledging and send the worst members packing. And every MP should adhere strictly to a self-denying ordinance, banning themselves from toadying. Some questions – even from clever, decent MPs – are just embarrassing. Take this from Bim Afolami, 'Does [the Prime Minister] agree that we need to do everything we can, whatever it takes, to stop sickening terrorist attacks taking place?'[5] What on earth did he expect him to reply? Or what about this from Fiona Bruce: 'Does the Prime Minister agree that the right way to secure the best future for the British people is to deliver on the people's priorities and secure a strong economy?'[6] I was thinking, 'For heaven's sake, you're a successful lawyer with your own firm. Is that really the best you can do?' I hope that one day a PM will say for sheer devilment, 'You know what? No, I don't. Blast the people's priorities and bugger a strong economy!'

PMQs will always be lively. And I defend the witty, well-placed heckle, which can cut a pompous minister down to size. After all, David Cameron said in his victory speech in 2010 that he was 'fed up with the Punch and Judy politics of Westminster, the name calling, backbiting, point scoring, finger pointing'. But he knew how important a clever quip could be. 'He was the future, once,' he told Blair.[7*]

THE REPUTATION OF 'HONOURABLE MEMBERS'

I want to issue one note of caution about this litany of parliamentary failings, though. I am painfully conscious that two of my colleagues, Jo Cox and Sir David Amess, have been murdered in recent years. Stirring up hatred of MPs does nobody any favours.

Yet all the scandals and bad behaviour have understandably made voters cynical about and contemptuous of MPs. I hear it all the time. 'Are you putting that on expenses, mate?' as you're scanning a pint of milk in Morrisons. Or 'You lot are only in it for yourselves.' Or 'You're all the same. If voting made any difference, you'd ban it.' Or, my favourite, especially when you're knocking on doors in torrential rain in the dark, your fingers raw with what feels like the onset of frostbite, 'Typical, you only ever come round when you want our votes.' Social media have exacerbated this tendency, giving voice to people's fury but rendering modern politics harsh, hateful and rebarbative. Twitter storms, Facebook pile-ons and email write-ins are the order of the day, often with little or no justification and

---

*Prime ministerial abuse has suffered a decline. When in Opposition, Lloyd George and Harold Wilson elegantly described their prime ministerial opponents as 'a shiver looking for a spine to run up' (a phrase recycled recently by Ian Blackford without attribution), but recent instances sound more like witless abuse: David Cameron called Ed Miliband a 'complete mug', 'a con man' and a 'waste of space' and Ed Balls a 'muttering idiot' and 'the most annoying person in modern politics'. Miliband in turn called Cameron 'the dunce of Downing Street', Major called Blair a 'dimwit' and Blair told Major, 'you are the weakest link, goodbye'.

even less chance of forcing someone to correct their lies. When the BBC analysed 3 million tweets mentioning MPs across a six-week period, they found that more than 3,000 offensive ones were sent every day and that 130,000 were 'toxic' in that they were intentionally, excessively and unreasonably rude and designed to force the MP to leave the conversation. At the lighter end of the scale men tend to be called 'moronic', 'an evil toad' or 'nazi', while women are accused of being 'thick', 'ignorant' or 'idiotic'. Gay men are 'perverts', 'nonces' or 'poofs'. The obloquy many face is vicious. Diane Abbott, for instance, has been the victim of appalling sustained trolling for years. Tories have faced the same. Alicia Kearns has been threatened with all forms of sexual violence. Maria Caulfield has tweeted that she has twice had her car tyres 'damaged with nails and screws'.[8] A fifty-six-year-old man, Ian Howgate, was convicted in November 2021 of 'waging a campaign of terror' against Laura Farris.[9] Endless threats, including from balaclava-wearing men outside his house, have meant the Conservative MP Stuart Anderson has had to move house, his children have needed police escorts and the Crown Prosecution Service has taken twelve individuals to court for threats made to him.

This aspect of modern politics has become so pervasive that MPs are fairly blasé about death threats. I was fairly certain that the guy who said he was going to attack me with a Cruise missile didn't possess one, for instance. But obsessed individuals can graduate into violence. One emailer sent me the following series of emails in one week: 'Your dead!!!!!!'; 'You are dead!!!!!!'; 'Your fckn dead! Has rishi had you arrested yet'; 'You are being arrested period you little cunt!!!!'; 'Il make sure your family pay!!! And it's public.....'; 'Youl die for good you cunt!!!!' The police have tried to track him down, but without success. It's fine to be blasé, but all of us are conscious that two men were imprisoned for plotting to kill the Labour MP Rosie Cooper.

Yes, we MPs individually and as a body absolutely need to regain the public's trust, but indiscriminate or vitriolic personal abuse aimed at MPs is not just hurtful, it is harmful and counter-productive. Online anonymity can give the vulnerable a voice, but it is daily abused to manufacture grievance and vitriol. I would love to see an end to it. If we are all permanently held in contempt without distinction, good people will never stand for parliament and cynical MPs will conclude that they might as well act contemptibly.

But – and it is a very big but – I cannot overstate how important it is that we restore a sense that standards matter in public life. Every time an MP downplays a colleague's serious misdemeanour or dismisses a story as 'Westminster tittle-tattle', they excuse bad behaviour and perilously damage the reputation of parliament. Every time a minister fails to answer a question, gives a misleading impression or fails to back their argument up with facts, they undermine the reputation of democratic politics.

I repeat – this is a very dangerous moment. The public think we've got this badly wrong. They distrust MPs, and distrust has a long half-life. They want a better brand of politics. They don't expect saints, but they want effective, competent, honest and accountable politicians who are manifestly inspired by public service. The polling is stark. A survey from July 2021 by the Constitution Unit at UCL found that 79 per cent of people thought that reform is needed so that politicians who do not act with integrity are punished. It's more than that, though. I fear that without radical treatment this wound will fester and putrefy. Heaven knows, there is plenty to be angry about in Britain today. Some concerns are completely legitimate – for instance about NHS backlogs and political cronyism. Some merely represent sharp political and ideological differences – witness the divide over Brexit or how to address poverty or tax the wealthy. But a new phenomenon has taken hold in recent years as conspiracy theories surrounding Covid, vaccines and migration, plus culture wars over LGBT+ equality, anti-racism and 'wokery' have added to a sense of bubbling resentment of the political system. It is utterly irresponsible to stir up this toxic brew, especially when social media provide a ready platform for political bile. So we must not be complacent. We cannot presume that democracy will resist the barrage of abuse it receives daily, and we have to remind ourselves that today's liberties and freedoms are easily lost, stolen or surrendered. Far from being a marginal concern, urgent reform of parliament and parliamentary conduct, so that our democracy inspires confidence and regains public trust, is essential. The alternative – an irretrievable collapse in support for democracy itself – is too hideous to countenance.

PARLIAMENT'S CRAZY PAVING

As the numbers show, this is indeed the worst parliament in our history. More than twenty MPs have been suspended or have left under a cloud. Rules have been flouted repeatedly, sometimes in plain sight. Ministers have lied and refused to correct the record, thereby rendering their lies deliberate. Try as it might, the government seems unable to escape the tar-baby of sleaze. And just when I think it's all going to calm down a bit, another scandal breaks.

One of the reasons we have found it difficult to deal with the misconduct of the 2019 parliament is that the system for promoting and enforcing standards in parliament and in government is not fit for purpose. Instead of a single organisation with a simple, clear code of conduct, we have a crazy paving of different bodies and rules that govern or regulate MPs. They more or less interlock, but often they overlap or leave vast gaps. That leaves MPs floundering and the public confused and exasperated.

One reason for this chaos is that the regulatory structure has evolved piecemeal and almost entirely in response to scandals or furores. The Register of Members' Financial Interests, for instance, largely owes its establishment to a visit to Greece in 1968 by (among others) the right-wing Labour MP Gordon Bagier, who claimed on his return to the UK that the dictatorial rule of the colonels was much misrepresented by the British press. In the resulting furore, Bagier admitted that he had been paid £500 for his services as a parliamentary consultant by the Fraser Public Relations company, which had a £100,000 contract with the Greek military regime. After denying that he had lobbied on their behalf, he escaped censure and went on to chair the Transport Select Committee. The register was duly created in 1974. Similarly, the Representation of the People Act 1981 (which automatically disqualifies an MP sentenced to imprisonment for more than a year) was hastily enacted following the election of the imprisoned IRA hunger striker Bobby Sands; the Standards and Privileges Committee, the parliamentary commissioner for standards and the Standards Committee sprang from the cash-for-questions row; the Recall of MPs Act and the creation of the Independent Parliamentary Standards Authority (IPSA) were a direct response to the expenses scandal of 2008/9; and the Independent Complaints and Grievance Scheme (ICGS) and the Independent Expert Panel which adjudicates on ICGS cases were a response to allegations in the wake of the #MeToo movement about bullying and sexual misconduct in parliament. And in case you think this is all ancient history, as I mentioned earlier, it is worth noting that we had a single Standards and Privileges Committee until 2013 but its work is now covered by three separate bodies. I know some MPs would object to lay members adjudicating on matters of parliamentary privilege (heaven forfend!), but do they really think solicitors, former chief constables and the like couldn't come to just as sensible and well-informed a view as MPs on whether a minister has lied recklessly or intentionally to parliament? Of course they could. Which is why we should re-merge Standards and Privileges into a single, consistent and coherent committee dealing with all forms of breaches apart from bullying, harassment and sexual misconduct (where it is important that MPs play no role and cannot undermine the total independence of the system).

There is no better example of this ad hominem (or ad scandalum) legislation than the House of Commons (Clergy Disqualification) Act 1801, which stipulated that 'No person ordained a priest or deacon, or being a minister of the Church of Scotland, shall be capable of being elected a member of the House of Commons.'[10] The government drew this up solely to expel one man: the very independently minded parliamentary reformer and anti-corruption campaigner John Horne Tooke, who had taken holy orders to please his father when he was young, but had devoted most of his life to politics and had just been returned for Old Sarum. Horne Tooke was a character. He had lost an eye in a school fight, he was put on trial for treason, he had an illegitimate family and responded when told to take a wife, 'With all my heart, whose wife shall it be?' Above all else, though, he was an irritant to the government, which changed the law to turf him out of parliament. It was an ill-conceived and confused law, later mildly ameliorated by the Clerical Disabilities Act 1870, which allowed Church of England priests and deacons to 'relinquish all rights, privileges, advantages, and exemptions of the office [of priest]', including the undoubted privilege of being excluded from parliament.[11] I used the 1870 Act to resign my orders so that I could stand in High Wycombe in 1997, but the 1801 Act was not repealed until David Cairns, who was a Catholic priest (and could not therefore avail himself of the 1870 Act), was selected for the then Labour seat of Greenock and Inverclyde in 2001. Thus the measure was both enacted and repealed in the interests of two men, 200 years apart.

Equally ludicrous is the fact that although 'resigning' as an MP sounds simple, it has been complicated thanks to two motions from the seventeenth century. The first was carried on Tuesday 2 March 1624 and states 'that a Man, after he is duly chosen, cannot relinquish'.[12] In other words, once elected, an MP cannot resign – a point most political novels irritatingly forget. The second motion, dating from December 1680, automatically disqualified an MP who received an 'Office, or Place of Profit, from the Crown'.[13] Thanks to the Succession to the Crown Act of 1707, this included ministers of the Crown, who had to face a by-election on appointment unless there had just been a general election. Ministerial by-elections were abolished in 1926, but the 1624 motion still stands. So, if you want a quick exit from the Commons and you can't wait for a general election, you have to go through the charmingly quaint legal fiction (or bizarre nonsense, depending on your general view of constitutional relics from a bygone era) of accepting one of the two posts that are reserved for this purpose, namely Crown steward and bailiff of the Chiltern Hundreds of Stoke, Desborough and Burnham; or the same office for the Manor of Northstead. It feels bitterly ironic when someone like Owen Paterson applies to the chancellor of the Exchequer for an 'office of profit' to avoid facing the music for financial misdeeds, but two other cases show how monstrously daft this is. Firstly, John Stonehouse, the Labour MP for Walsall North, applied for the Chiltern Hundreds when he was arrested in Melbourne in 1974 (after faking his own death to run off with his secretary and avoid mounting debts), but refused to sign the relevant papers, so remained an MP while being extradited, while on remand in Brixton Prison and while on bail, and even made a personal statement to the Commons supposedly explaining his actions in October 1975, but only finally accepted the Chiltern Hundreds on 27 August 1976, three weeks after being convicted and sentenced to seven years in prison.[*] Likewise, the Sinn Fein MP Gerry Adams wrote to the government in 2011 in the following terms: 'A chara [Dear friend], I hereby resign as MP for the constituency of west Belfast. Go raibh maith agat [thank you]. Gerry Adams.'[14] He then complained when George Osborne,

---

[*] Just to complicate matters, he was convicted of a 'misdemeanour' rather than a 'felony' (which would have automatically excluded him).

as chancellor, appointed him as Crown steward of the Chiltern Hundreds, saying 'I am an Irish republican. I have had no truck whatsoever with these antiquated and quite bizarre aspects of the British parliamentary system.'[15] It seemed the law was on his side, as the 1975 House of Commons Disqualification Act states that no MP 'shall be required to accept any office or place by virtue of which he would be disqualified by this Act for membership of that House'.[16] But, if that were the case, he had as a republican no legal means of resigning, so a legal fudge was created whereby the chancellor merely assumed that any request to resign was deemed a request to be appointed and disqualified and the Speaker declared the seat vacant. Clearly the whole system is a nonsense, and its reform is long overdue.

It's the same when it comes to the gallimaufry of codes governing MPs' behaviour. Admittedly, the Code of Official Conduct and the Ethics Manual of the US House of Representatives runs to 408 pages. But today's MPs have to abide by the following: the standing orders of the House; the Code of Conduct and Guide to the Rules; the Ministerial Code; the Parliamentary Behaviour Code (which lays down the behaviour expected of all members of both Houses and the whole parliamentary community); the Stationery Rules; the All-Party Parliamentary Groups Rules; the Rules of Behaviour and Courtesies in the House of Commons; the Speaker's rules on the use of the crowned portcullis (the special emblem that denotes the authority of the House); the rules of IPSA; and the oath of office. Their conduct is regulated or overseen by the standards commissioner and registrar; the Committee on Standards; the Committee of Privileges; the Independent Complaints and Grievance Scheme; the Independent Expert Panel;

the Electoral Commission; the independent adviser on ministers' interests; the Advisory Committee on Business Appointments; the Committee on Standards in Public Life; and the Speaker. In addition, they can be disqualified or unseated under the Forfeiture Act 1870, the Insolvency Act 1986, the Enterprise Act 2002 and the Recall of MPs Act 2015 or thanks to an election petition.*

Each political party also has its own disciplinary processes. These are shrouded in confidentiality. Some allegations about MPs' conduct are made solely to the relevant party, which will normally suspend the whip from the member pending investigation. It is understandable that parties want to protect their reputation by enforcing discipline – but frivolous or vexatious complaints that are left unresolved for months can lead to an MP being unfairly suspended and unable to stand at a general election, which is why Sir Charles Walker claims that 'MPs have fewer rights than anyone else in Britain.' Sometimes a complainant will shop around and only go to the party if they have failed to get the police or the ICGS to take their complaint. This is manifestly unfair. Much greater transparency is required – and a clear commitment to due process, timeliness and a fair hearing. I would also like to see all the political parties adopt a shared protocol for dealing with such complaints. Otherwise, political parties expose their MPs to the settling of scores via pseudo-judicial processes.

It's no excuse for bad behaviour, but this is a right old hotch-potch of disciplinary bodies and processes, and at times it feels as if the left hand doesn't know what the

---

*An outline of the main regulatory bodies affecting MPs is included on pp. 207–9.

right hand is doing. For instance, why oh why does a breach of the Ministerial Code not also count as a breach of the parliamentary Code of Conduct? Why do we think that it's the end of the matter if a minister has been sacked for leaking secret information or bullying their civil servants or breaching their own Covid rules? Should these breaches not also automatically be investigated by the parliamentary commissioner for standards as breaches of the Code of Conduct and, if necessary, incur further sanction? After all, the public doesn't draw such neat and tidy distinctions. They see ministers and MPs as politicians, pure and simple. So the rules should apply equally and equally fairly to all. As things stand, the network of bodies amounts to less than the sum of its parts. It is confusing, it is full of inconsistencies and it undermines accountability and transparency. The public doesn't understand it and MPs are terrified of tripping up unintentionally. It is not fit for purpose and it is in severe need of reform. At the very least we need to align the rules for the Commons and the Lords and combine the Code of Conduct and the Ministerial Code (and all the other codes), which should be overseen by a single independent parliamentary standards body. There should be no loopholes that excuse bad behaviour just because an MP was acting 'in a ministerial capacity'. A breach of the Ministerial Code should constitute a breach of the Code of Conduct – and vice versa.

Combining bodies and amalgamating codes will not be easy. Some think the fundamental problem is that MPs 'mark their own homework'. And it is true that the House of Commons has long asserted its sole right (often referred to as its 'exclusive cognisance') to discipline its members without the interference of the courts, for the very good reason that unless the MP has committed and been convicted of a criminal offence, only a democratically elected body should be able to overturn the decision of the voters in a particular constituency by suspending, expelling or otherwise limiting the actions of a duly elected MP. But we cannot continue like this. We need simple, clear, intelligible, straightforward rules that apply equally to all. We need due process and a fair hearing. We need consistency rather than caprice.

But I'm getting ahead of myself. This is not just about individual behaviour, or about structures and processes. It's about a culture and a set of systemic problems with how we do politics in this country which erode public trust and render government and parliament dysfunctional. We all focus on the glaring headlines of the separate scandals. But I contend that there is something far more significant we need to address next – the extraordinary stranglehold on power that our system gives the prime minister and their government from the moment they arrive in Downing Street. Ministers, of course, see no problem with it. They think it is the natural order. But it is dangerous, pernicious and a massive fault line in our brand of democracy.

2

The Winner Takes It All

The Liberal MP for West Ham North, Edward Rider Cook, was a soap manufacturer, so perhaps his nose was more sensitive than others, but on 27 May 1886 he told the Commons, 'I do not rise ... to take part in the discussion upon the amendment before the committee, but to call attention to the abominable atmosphere in which we are sitting. It seems to me that the air of this House is not only disagreeable, but that we are really sitting here at the risk of our lives.'[1] The issue was the drains and the answer was a great pump designed by Isaac Shone that would spit the contents of the palace drains up into Joseph Bazalgette's magnificent new sewers next to Westminster Bridge. Lots of people visit Big Ben to see the clock, but for my money the 'pneumatic sewage ejector' that sits beneath it is just as impressive. It's a vast cast-iron sphere in the 'Torpedo Room' deep underground beneath a tiny patch of grass known as the Speaker's Green. It's been in constant operation since 1887 and, although you get a whiff of something not quite right as you descend the narrow flight of stairs, it hasn't failed us yet. (You may be wondering why I know about the palace drains. As deputy leader of the House in 2008–9 and chair of the Finance Committee in 2017–19, I paid regular visits to the Torpedo Room because we worried just as much about a catastrophic event in the basement as about a fire in the attic. Either could easily close parliament for months.)

Some think the same of the UK's famously unwritten (but actually partly written) constitution. They claim it hasn't failed us yet, that because it proceeds by evolution, not revolution, it protects us from autocracy and capricious government and ensures that we are about as odour-free as a nation can be. I disagree. To my mind there is a distinct smell about the place – and it's time we dug the drains up. I'm no Marxist, but we definitely need a revolution in the way we do things. Because in truth we citizens of this sceptred isle have persuaded ourselves for far too long that Britain is clean and pure, that the 'Old Corruption' of rotten and pocket boroughs is a thing of the distant past, that our parliamentary system is clean (if not quite immaculate) and that we are not like dictatorships or banana republics, where political pets win prizes. And yes, we have the trappings of democracy: elections, the rule of law, a constitutional monarchy fettered by statute, an independent judiciary. That's why we tell ourselves – and teach our children – that the rule of law is sacrosanct in Britain, and that our elections are free and fair. But it's time we stopped kidding ourselves. Britain is not *steeped* in corruption. Ministers aren't enriching themselves at taxpayers' expense like Putin or Imelda Marcos (although ex-premiers can certainly afford a roomful of smart shoes). But complacency, effortless Great British superiority and false assumptions about the effectiveness of checks on ministerial power mean our country is losing its footing on the moral high ground. Rather like the Venetians, whose doges carried on celebrating the ancient glories of 'La Serenissima' by sailing out into the lagoon and wedding the sea with a jewelled ring long after their dominance of the Adriatic had evaporated, we polish our democratic medallions, we boast of being the 'mother of parliaments' and we rarely dare to examine our own failings. But this is a fool's paradise and every idiot knows that a fool's paradise is a paradise only for fools.

Let me be clear. I'm not talking (at this point) about whether and to what extent the UK and its government are corrupt. That is for the next chapter, when we look at the actions of ministers. Nor am I talking about the deeds and misdeeds of individuals. We will come to those later, too. No, first we need to look at the underlying structural problem in our British way of doing politics, so we must dig up the drains, as it were. We must scrutinise the way our system works and the power it gives to the government of the day. This has always been my primary beef, because the dominant theme of the British constitution is, to paraphrase ABBA, 'the winner takes it all, the loser's standing small'. Ministers rule. The Opposition – and, for that matter backbench government MPs – are impotent and are left to growl. This overarching principle is buttressed by two assumptions. Firstly, all government ministers must be a member of one or other House of parliament;[*] and secondly, a prime minister gets to form the government because they enjoy the confidence of the House of Commons. This is simple, it's clear and in the main it's fine. It means that all ministers are accountable to parliament and that the party that wins more than half of the seats in the Commons gets to govern. This is, some argue, democracy in action. True, our electoral system

---

[*]This is not written in any law, but is the accepted convention.

doesn't accurately or proportionally reflect the nation and the electorate doesn't always give a clear verdict – the 2010 and 2017 elections gave no party an absolute majority, for instance – but in the main it delivers the people's choice of government.

This tidiness has a downside, though, because once your party have won a general election and you are the prime minister, as long as you retain your majority in the Commons (however nebulously that is expressed), you can pretty much do what you want in parliament. You alone appoint or dismiss ministers; dole out honours and seats in the Lords; determine if and when parliament sits, when it goes into recess or is prorogued* and what legislation it considers; set the date of a general election; lay out the machinery of government; and determine every penny of taxation and expenditure. You can use your majority to alter or suspend the standing orders of the Commons at will (even, for instance, barring some MPs from voting on certain measures). Only a government minister appointed by you can table an amendment to vary a duty or a tax, only a minister can table the date for a parliamentary recess, only your bills and motions get precedence on the order paper and only your government amendments are guaranteed to be considered and adopted when the time you have allocated for debate runs out.

A single historical moment shows how things have degenerated. One of the political rows on the eve of the Second World War was over the seemingly minor

---

*The power to prorogue parliament is significant. Prorogation suspends parliament for a period and ends the parliamentary session, thereby ditching all uncompleted business such as public or private members' bills and unanswered written questions. No committees may meet nor parliamentary questions to ministers be tabled when parliament is prorogued.

question of whether the Commons should be suspended for a long summer recess in 1939, as the prime minister Neville Chamberlain wanted. Some MPs who opposed his policy of appeasement feared he would do a deal with Hitler if parliament were not sitting, so they tabled an amendment demanding a shorter recess and an earlier return of the Commons. They lost (and it all proved immaterial when Hitler invaded Poland), but at least they were allowed to table and vote on an amendment. Nowadays, thanks to a government change to the standing orders, no such amendment is allowed. Only ministers decide even minor things like this, because ministers are omnipotent. That is a phenomenal concentration of power. And power, like money and muck, is best spread around.

It isn't absolute power. Your backbenchers might knock you off course, as might the House of Lords. The Human Rights Act of 1998 might limit your scope, as might the courts (unless you manage to neuter them, as many casual or experienced autocrats seek to do). But it is, to use a term first coined to sum up the policies of the Italian revolutionary general Giuseppe Garibaldi and repeated by Lord Hailsham (when he was in opposition in 1976), an 'elective dictatorship'. It is problematic because in a fully functioning constitutional monarchy, government is only ever by consent. The voters lend elected representatives their authority to make laws, tax, spend and govern the nation. They even allow us to deprive people of their liberty, seize their property and go to war, in the wider public interest, to prevent crime and in the name of national security. At the heart of that relationship is trust. Elected politicians 'dressed in a little brief authority' (as Isabella puts it in *Measure for Measure*) hold their positions temporarily in trust. As the former Speaker of the US House of Representatives, Henry Clay, said, 'Government is a trust, and the officers of the government are trustees. And both the trust and the trustees are created for the benefit of the people.'[2] The inference is clear. Every time the public's trust is abused, whimsically, recklessly or deliberately, the institutions that are meant to protect our freedoms are undermined. Representative democracy is handed down through the generations like a family heirloom and we can either burnish it or tarnish it. What we cannot do is presume upon it. Which is why the way we govern, the way we do business in parliament, the way government rules us and the extent of government's power are all things that matter.

Here's the problem. Unlike the US system, which was deliberately created with substantial checks and balances to the power of the executive, much of what keeps British government on the strait and narrow[*] is not written in a constitution or even in statute law but is framed by convention and gentleman's agreement. But gentlemen's agreements are easily ignored – especially if those in power aren't really gentlemen. And conventions last only as long as the strongest-willed person in the room subscribes to them. Our system for calling an early general election, for instance, has been called a 'good guys' charter' (with apologies for the casual sexism) because it presumes that the prime minister will always act honourably in the national interest. Yet Boris Johnson's illegal prorogation of parliament in 2019, when he sought the Queen's permission to suspend parliament for an unusually prolonged period for his own partisan

---

[*]I know, 'strait and narrow' seems a tautology, but it is the original, deriving from 'strait is the gate, and narrow is the way, which leadeth unto life' (Matthew 7:14).

and Brexit-related reasons, shows we cannot always make such an assumption. You can't normally rely on a gentleman's agreement in a court of law, nor should we for our checks and balances on the power of the executive, aka the government. No, the winner should not always take it all. In the words of the Sugababes, that's a 'one-way ticket to a madman's destination'.

We can only protect good government in the UK if we put stronger, more effective checks and balances in place, such as requiring a two-thirds majority for changes to standing orders, or a legal requirement for the civil service to be independent. In theory that's the role of the courts and parliament, but under 'winner takes all' even these are neutered. Every voter and taxpayer in the land has a stake in this. If politicians get away with lying or nepotism, our national reputation for financial reliability will be harmed, we will become a less safe bet for international investors and our economy will suffer. If we constantly excuse bad behaviour in politics, we risk authoritarian politicians exploiting public cynicism to dismantle the architecture of democracy. And if we continue to place all the levers of power exclusively and without restriction in the hands of ministers, we risk them abusing their position, manipulating the system and abrogating yet more power to themselves. That could all too easily create a vicious circle towards authoritarianism. That is why I completely disagree with Churchill's oft-quoted comment (made in 1947 when the voters had chucked him out) that 'democracy is the worst form of government – except all those other forms that have been tried from time to time'.[3] Admittedly, he went on to say 'there is the broad feeling in our country that the people should rule, continuously rule, and that public opinion, expressed by all constitutional means, should shape, guide, and control the actions of Ministers who are their servants and not their masters', but I fear his apparent scepticism about democracy has seized too many people's imaginations.[4] I've seen what dictators do. I lived in Argentina not long after the Falklands War and saw the 'hospitals' where trades unionists were tortured with electric cattle prods. I saw Chilean police prevent the funeral of a lad who had been set on fire by Pinochet's police, when water cannons and tear gas made in Britain were used to disperse the congregation. I've stood in a hideout in eastern Ukraine and watched Russian snipers take aim at civilians. I've met Argentine and Iranian campaigners who've been beaten, poisoned and imprisoned for disagreeing with their government. And I know one thing for sure. Democracy is a precious thing, but it is fragile. It means being able to decide your country's future, it means protecting minority opinions, it means being able to combine with others to create change, it means never being completely powerless. Someone can always find a reason why autocracy is simpler, more efficient, more resilient. But we should, we *must*, block our ears to those siren voices. Democracy – free, fair, open, honest, well-informed democracy – was worth fighting for in the air, on the sea and in the trenches of two world wars. It is worth defending, refreshing and reinvigorating today.

After all, according to *Democracy Index*, a regular report produced by the Economist Group, there has been 'a decline and stagnation in democracy around the world' in recent years, and roughly four in ten people around the world live under authoritarian regimes where 'democracy' is at best a sham.[5] The remaining 60 per cent live under some form of democracy. Systems vary. Some are presidential, others parliamentary. Some presidents are powerful, others are little more than a figurehead. Some have more frequent elections than others. They come at least every three years in New Zealand and Australia and members of the US House of Representatives are up for re-election every two years, whereas a UK parliament can last for five years from first sitting to dissolution. Hence the last date for the next general election is 24 January 2025. (I have always thought five years is too long. Most governments run out of steam and the public starts clamouring for an election long before then, which is why four years makes more sense.) There are other differences. Some democracies have written constitutions, which guarantee minority and individual rights. But the basic principle is that the people – all the people – get to vote and choose their government. Some think that is the end of the matter. That's basically the modern Tory view. They claim that every nation needs the smack of firm government, so there should be very few limits to the powers of government between elections. I disagree. Just because you hold the reins of power doesn't mean you should be able to drive off in any direction you choose. After all, once elected, authoritarians have often used the democratic reins of power to drive democracy into a ditch – and continue to do so, most notably in the Russian Federation and, arguably, in Poland and Hungary.

Part of the problem is the government's complete control over business in the House of Commons. Jacob Rees-Mogg thinks this is essential to the smooth running of government. 'The whole point of the Government having control of the timetable is that that is an expression of confidence,' he says.[6] But it wasn't always like that. Up until the nineteenth century the Commons regulated its timetable and order paper, but throughout the Victorian era government steadily encroached on this preserve. First it took control of Tuesdays and Fridays, then it seized the rest of the week. Since the beginning of the twentieth century, the prime minister and their appointed leader of the House totally command the timetable and the order paper. Government business has precedence all day every day (except when the Speaker uses specific powers to grant an urgent question, an emergency debate or a privileges motion) and even backbench business sessions, Opposition Days (when an opposition party gets to decide the motion for debate) and private members' bills days are allocated by the government. The allocation of time has got far worse in recent years. In theory the government and Opposition whips (normally euphemistically referred to as 'the usual channels') agree timetabling, but as often as not nowadays the government proceeds with what it wants to do regardless. Time is a government's greatest political weapon. A government with a threadbare legislative agenda will deliberately allocate too much time to marginal uncontroversial measures, in order to look busy, but will allow much less time to controversial bills. The result is the House often draws stumps early – and gets told off by the House of Lords when we do not debate draft laws properly. Government also likes to keep its cards very close to its chest, which is why it announces business only a week in advance (or two at most). This means MPs' and ministers' forward diaries are often works of fiction and politicians frequently have to cancel long-scheduled events because the business is changed at the last minute (which irritates constituents no end, undermines public confidence and makes it difficult for MPs to have stable family relationships).

THE WINNER TAKES IT ALL

THE SHAMEFUL WAY WE MAKE LAWS

Law-making is at the heart of governing, so let's start with primary legislation, that is to say, bills that become acts of parliament. In theory every Bill goes through several stages in each House: first reading (i.e. publication and laying before parliament); second reading (a general debate on the floor of the House); committee stage, when the Bill and any amendments are considered line by line either in committee or in a committee of the whole House; report stage, when amendments can again be considered in a committee of the whole House; and third reading (another general debate and vote on the amended Bill, plus, in the Lords, another chance to consider amendments). The process normally takes several months but it can be speeded through in an emergency (or whenever the government feels like it). It sounds elegant and thorough and sometimes it works perfectly. But recent experience has been scandalous.

Consider the National Security Bill, which started life in the Commons on 11 May 2022. At committee stage the government tabled a whole new section creating a Foreign Influence Registration scheme, and added eighty-one amendments, new clauses and new schedules at report stage. Many of these created new offences or significantly curbed personal freedom. Yet the government had set down that the whole Bill including report stage and third reading had to be completed by 7 p.m. Thanks to two urgent questions (demanded by backbench MPs and granted by the Speaker) and two government statements, the House did not start consideration of the Bill until 4.03, so it had less than two hours to consider forty-seven pages of amendments. MPs were allowed just four minutes each to express concerns. Four votes (each taking 13–15 minutes) meant that third reading of the first National Security Bill in many years was allowed just nine minutes of debate. Because government (and only government) amendments must be decided at the end of the allocated time, seventy-five of the government's changes to its own Bill were agreed without debate or vote. Such a deliberate use of the allocation of time to stifle debate is an arrogation of power and we would rightly condemn any other country that treated scrutiny of national security legislation so cursorily.

The same happened with the Illegal Immigration Bill. By the home secretary's own admission, it may break international and national law. It may be struck down by the courts for being in breach of our international obligations. So it is evidently controversial. Dozens of MPs wanted to speak in the second reading debate on 13 March 2023 – both against and in favour, on both sides of the House. You might think that that would mean it would get at least a full day's debate, if not two. But yet again the government decided to make two unprompted statements that afternoon, deliberately taking up debating time, so that the House started on the Bill two hours late at 5.45 p.m., allowing just over four hours before the votes at 10. That's just over sixteen seconds for each of the 980 desperate migrants found crossing the Channel in a small boat in January (which is the issue the Bill is supposed to tackle). Why should we care? Because laws have a real impact on people's lives and we must spend time getting them right. Otherwise we end up with bad, poorly drafted, ill-conceived laws, laws that have to be repealed or amended within months – and it's how ministers get away with poor decision-making.

Even worse is the fact that government has phenomenal powers thanks to provisions in primary legislation that allow ministers to introduce secondary or delegated legislation in the form of 'regulations' known as 'statutory instruments'.* The Childcare Act 2016, for instance, is a skeletal act of just seven short sections with very little of substance apart from eleven new powers granted to ministers to change the rules governing childcare, including the power to create new criminal offences, impose financial penalties and 'amend, repeal or revoke any provision made by or under an Act (whenever passed or made)' – all by regulations.[7] Amazingly, any such regulations stemming from this or any other Act of parliament are unamendable and many don't even have to be approved in parliament before they become law. In other words, once the government has used its Commons majority to give itself secondary powers, it can exercise them to its heart's content.

This was never more obvious than during Covid. Between the start of the pandemic and March 2022 the government drew on 131 acts of parliament for 582 of these regulations. Many imposed very significant restrictions on personal liberty, enforcing lockdowns, forbidding travel, closing businesses, requiring tests and introducing hefty fines for non-compliance. Only thirty of them were debated *at all* before they came into force. As many as 228 breached the parliamentary rule that that they should be published twenty-one days before they come into force. What's more, 13 per cent came into force *before* they were even published and,

---

*The most egregious of these (which allow ministers to amend the original legislation) are known as 'Henry VIII powers', as they mirror the Statute of Proclamations of 1539, whereby parliament gave Henry VIII the right to bypass parliament and pass laws directly.

in some cases, legally enforceable rules – for instance mandating the use of face masks – were in place for a whole month before they were laid before parliament, i.e. published. Whether you agreed with lockdowns or not, the parliamentary means of introducing them was little short of tyranny. No MP could table changes to a single one. The Commons, and the country, had to like it or lump it. National emergencies and global pandemics may necessitate swift action, but the lack of due scrutiny undermined public confidence because it became abundantly clear that not even ministers understood their own rules.

Bringing up the rear in this legislative trilogy of parliamentary inadequacy is the system of private members' bills (PMBs). Let me explain – and bear with me. Most new laws start life as public bills tabled by the government, but backbench MPs have three ways of introducing bills: they can enter the PMBs ballot at the start of each session of parliament, they can submit a ten-minute-rule bill or they can table a presentation bill. If an MP comes high up in the ballot their Bill will get one of the top spots on one of thirteen Fridays every session when the standing orders provide that the House sits. If the MP chooses wisely and plays their cards right (selecting a non-contentious, popular measure and buttering up the government), they stand a decent chance of getting their Bill on to the statute books. Ten-minute-rule bills (which are so called because the MP speaks for only ten minutes and can be opposed for ten minutes) are less likely to make it, as are presentation bills (which are merely bills published by an individual MP and laid before the House but never debated), as they join the back of the Friday queue and might never be debated again. In all, 377 PMBs gained royal assent between 1983 and December 2022. Just sixteen were ten-minute-rule bills and not one was a presentation bill. Only seventy-nine opposition MPs have managed to get a bill through since 1983 – and a sign of how this has deteriorated is that only fourteen have done so since 2010.

The system seems promising. An individual MP gets to make a difference. But all that glitters is not gold. PMB Fridays are fraught with problems. For a start, most MPs are back in their constituencies, so there is no certainty about who will be present and some really irritating MPs dominate proceedings as if the whole thing is a game. Sometimes an MP with a good cause will try and persuade their mates to turn up, even though they know their Bill is going nowhere, either because the government opposes it or because they are too far down the list. This is particularly frustrating when someone runs a noisy social media campaign on the Bill and MPs' inboxes fill up with hundreds of emails demanding we attend – when we all know for a fact that the Bill is going absolutely nowhere and may not even be debated.

Then there's the 'object' moment. Right at the end of a Friday sitting a clerk will read out one by one the names of each of the bills that haven't yet been debated. If nobody objects as each bill is mentioned, it will get its second reading and be sent to committee to be debated line by line. If, however, a single MP shouts 'object' when a specific bill is named, it goes back to the end of the queue for next time. One self-righteous MP delights in doing this – Sir Christopher Chope. His most famous intervention came in 2018 when the Liberal Democrat MP Wera Hobhouse was hoping that nobody would object to her Voyeurism (Offences) Bill, which would have banned the taking of surreptitious sexually intrusive photographs. She even had the support of the government minister, Lucy Frazer. All it needed was for Chope to shut up. We were assured someone had sat on him (metaphorically). But he shouted 'object' and the Bill went to the back of the queue again. The hypocrisy is that he tabled forty-seven bills of his own that year, deliberately clogging up the system so that other bills were blocked.

However, the bigger problem with PMBs is government interference. Far from letting things proceed unimpeded, the government of the day takes a keen interest. It gives 'hand-out' bills to loyal government members. These are normally minor amendments to the law that the government cannot be bothered to table in its own time. In Charles Walker's words they are 'worthy but boring'.[8] One such was John Glen's Merchant Shipping (Homosexual Conduct) Act 2017, which stopped homosexuality from being a legal reason for dismissal from the crew of a merchant ship. I supported it, but it consisted of two short clauses and could easily have been added to another government bill. Another was the Local Government (Disqualification) Act 2022, which bars people who are subject to orders due to sexual offences (such as a requirement to notify the local authorities if they move house) from standing for or remaining in office, to which nobody objected. Feeble MPs love hand-outs, but I understand why they take them, because the rules mean that Friday is also the only time when a bill the government opposes can be talked out. The day starts at 9.30 a.m., but if a member is still speaking on a bill at 2.30 p.m., it is carried forward to another date, without making any progress. Rather than embarrass themselves by voting down a popular proposal, government whips persuade ultra-loyal colleagues in search of a ministerial job to come along and speak endlessly so that the measure withers. (I did it once. Never again.) Without government support, the member in charge of the Bill is left like a party in the *Bleak House* case of Jarndyce vs Jarndyce, attending week after week and never getting a resolution. This can lead to ludicrous parliamentary manoeuvres. That is what happened with Barry Gardiner's Bill in 2021 to ban the practice of 'fire and rehire', also known as the Employment and Trade Union Rights (Dismissal and Re-engagement) Bill. After government members deliberately hung around in the division lobbies for twenty minutes during a vote on whether the House should meet in private (until the Deputy Speaker sent the serjeant at arms in his tights and with his sword to 'clear the lobbies'), Barry was allowed to start at 9.52 and faced endless interventions from Tories trying to keep him speaking. The health minister Maggie Throup made an unscheduled and vacuous statement on the government's 'mission to help people live healthier lives' at 11 and only faced questions from Tory MPs (again trying to waste time).[9] The Opposition was allowed a closure motion by the Deputy Speaker at 1.20 p.m., which the Tories voted down, so when the minister Paul Scully started speaking at 1.40 p.m., he only had to keep going for fifty minutes before he – and the Bill – hit the buffers. It's not by chance that the name for this – filibustering – comes from a nineteenth-century Spanish word for pirate.

The PMB system isn't a complete waste of time. In the 1960s the government helped Sydney Silverman (Labour), David Steel (Liberal), Humphry Berkeley (Conservative) and Leo Abse (Labour) steer the end of the death penalty, the legalisation of abortion and the partial legalisation of homosexuality on to the statute books as PMBs. Some excellent modern bills have got through, including Cheryl Gillan's Autism Act 2009, Sarah Wollaston's Stalking Protection Act 2019 and my own Assaults on Emergency Workers (Offences) Act 2018. However, the Friday shenanigans mean the process misleads the public and wastes the House's time. I would introduce three reforms. Firstly, move PMBs to Tuesday evenings once a month after the main business, so that all MPs are freer to take part. Secondly, guarantee every bill a second reading vote after three hours (and thereby end filibustering). If the government doesn't like a bill, the least it can do is show its hand and vote it down. Thirdly, allow the House (rather the government) to decide what happens to a bill that gets a second reading. Sir Charles Walker, who was then chair of the Procedure Committee, complained in 2016 that 'the Private Member's Bill process is in total disrepute' and that the government was in the 'last-chance saloon',[10] but sadly nothing has changed since then, largely because government likes it that way. The danger is that the same could apply even if we changed government. Again, I can hear you cry, 'So what?' But I would argue that this parliamentary nonsense infantilises MPs. It puts too much power in the hands of ministers. It renders parliament incomprehensible. And it leads to countless dashed hopes and false dawns.

RAISING MONEY — AND SPENDING IT

The 'winner takes all' principle (and the consequent almost total irrelevance of parliament) also applies to government expenditure over which the Commons (rather than the Lords) has exclusive rights. For a start we don't have an annual budget in the proper sense of the word, with income and expenditure laid beside one another and open to amendment and debate. Unlike every local authority in the land, we just have a Budget statement, in which the government announces its broad economic strategy. Any changes it proposes to taxes and duties are agreed in the 'Budget approval motions' and a finance bill, but expenditure is managed separately via the 'main estimates', which the government publishes for all departments soon after the start of the financial year. Parliament allocates only two days of debate (i.e. at most twelve hours) for four of these departmental estimates in June or July. These four estimates can be amended, but only downwards, while the vast majority of remaining departmental estimates are agreed without any debate whatsoever through the innocuously entitled 'roll-up supply motions', which cannot be amended up or down. This concentration of absolute power over the nation's purse-strings derives from a motion of 1713 that 'this House will receive no Petition for any sum of money relating to public services but what is recommended from the Crown',[11] but it means that if the 'Crown' (aka the government) changes its mind, it can have as many additional budgets, autumn statements or 'fiscal events' as it wants (as we saw in 2022). I'm not arguing for the Lords to play a role in agreeing expenditure, but the fact that the Commons does this so badly is a pernicious scandal.

This process has the semblance of scrutiny, but it is a sham. If the Opposition thinks the government's proposed increase in the state pension, for instance, is too low, all it can do is make a speech complaining about it. It can't table a higher increase. If it votes against the government's departmental estimate for

Work and Pensions because it thinks welfare payments are too stingy, it is voting against all that department's expenditure. The same applies to the annual police and local government grants. A classic example of this came when the government cut the police grant. The Labour Party (then led by Jeremy Corbyn) decided to vote against the grant in 2017 to signal that we disagreed with the cut. But now the home secretary Suella Braverman claims (with a sliver of truth) that Labour has voted against funding the police. A more sensible system would allow all MPs to table amendments to vary estimates up and down. (Incidentally, for those who are interested in the House of Commons' own finances, including its expenditure on food and catering, there is also a parliamentary administration estimate, which is also unamendable and is rolled up with all the others. This means MPs could not vote to end subsidies of the catering outlets without closing down parliament.)

For all these reasons, it is time the Commons took back control of its timetable, the order paper and the process of raising and spending taxpayers' money, as is common in most other parliamentary democracies. This was recommended by the Select Committee on Reform of the House of Commons chaired by Tony Wright in 2009 and was promised by the coalition government in 2010, but never implemented. In particular, the House should elect a business committee to draw up the weekly agenda, which should be subject to amendment and a vote. A few other simple measures would help. Prorogation and dissolution of parliament should only be allowed following a vote of the Commons; recess and prorogation motions should be amendable; no secondary legislation should come into force before it is published; and no amendments to a bill, including government amendments, should be agreed after a time limit imposed through the government's programme or allocation of time motion (often referred to as 'the knives' or 'guillotine') has expired. Ministers, armed equally with self-importance and a sense of entitlement, hate scrutiny. They try to swat it away like an irritating fly. They like the 'winner takes all' principle. But it fosters complacency, laziness and a culture of impunity. Relatively minor changes to our standing orders would sharpen ministerial attention, improve scrutiny, prevent some of the worst decisions and force ministers to treat all MPs as adults rather than spoon-fed toddlers.

RIGGING THE PARLIAMENTARY ARITHMETIC

The 'winner takes all' principle reaches deep into our constitutional psyche. Government doesn't just have total control of how we do our business in parliament. It also controls key elements of the composition of parliament itself. Let's deal with the Commons first. Whatever you think about our first-past-the-post electoral system (I would prefer a proportional or additional-member system), we have tended to presume that modern British elections are fair and free. I am not convinced. It is a scandal that, despite the legal requirement that one should register to vote, more than 9 million people are not registered at their current address (or anywhere). Most of them are poorer, younger or from ethnic minorities. You might have thought that any government that did not want to abuse its trust would seek to encourage everyone to register by making the process simpler and using other government data sets to ensure the electoral register is as complete and accurate as possible. But the government

has set itself against any such measures and its Elections
Act of 2022 not only fails to tackle under-registration but
will make it more difficult for those same groups to vote,
by insisting that voters present photo ID at the ballot
box, supposedly to prevent voter fraud. Leaving aside
the hypocrisy of not requiring photo ID to vote in a
Conservative leadership contest, this has a double benefit
for the Conservatives. The groups that under-register are
more likely to vote Labour, and, unusually in the west,
we in the UK draw constituency boundaries on the basis
of registered voters rather than population. This means
that when ethnic minorities and younger voters in inner
cities fail to register, seats are redistributed from urban
areas to rural areas, from Labour to Conservative. In
other words, the government is making it more difficult
for potential Labour voters to vote and is gerrymandering
seats to its advantage.* This is the very same strategy that
Trump and his allies have used in the US.

The one fly in the government's ointment has been
the Electoral Commission, which was set up as an
independent body in 2000 to regulate the funding
of political parties and elections and to set standards
for running elections and referendums. It has clearly
antagonised government ministers, frequently opposing
their legislation and fining the Conservative Party
(for instance for failing to declare Lord Brownlow's
£67,801.72 donation to redecorate Downing Street for
Johnson in 2020). When the government proposed

---

*'Gerrymandering' is a portmanteau word that comes from Governor Elbridge
Gerry who in 1812 signed off new boundaries for Massachusetts State seats
that had been deliberately drawn up to spread support for the Republicans and
concentrate their opponents' votes, thereby giving the Republicans a significant
electoral advantage. When the editor of the *Boston Gazette* saw a map showing
the shape of the new Essex seat, he said, 'Salamander! Call it a Gerrymander.'

changing the legislation at the start of 2022 to enable ministers to draw up the 'strategy and policy statement' for the Electoral Commission, all its board members (apart from the Tory peer Stephen Gilbert) wrote to say that this was 'inconsistent with the role that an independent electoral commission plays in a healthy democracy'.[12] Yet the government ploughed on.

And then there's the House of Lords. I don't know whether it is a British love of pomp and circumstance (don't we do state occasions well?) or a nostalgic admiration for the past, but we often ignore quite how bonkers our parliament is in retaining a very powerful second chamber consisting of 668 appointed life peers, 91 elected hereditary peers (I know, quite beyond explanation) and 26 lords spiritual (i.e. Church of England bishops). Defending the composition of the Lords requires an infinite capacity for doublethink, and I have long campaigned for a wholly or substantially elected second chamber on the grounds that nobody should have a legislative job for life and the least you should do if you want to help govern the country is face election. I know many colleagues disagree. They claim (I think spuriously) that, by virtue of being unelected, peers can be less partisan; and (more convincingly) that two elected Houses might rival each other and lead to gridlock unless their respective powers were laid down in statute. But my main point here is that uniquely in any major democracy the British government of the day has a simple means of altering the composition of parliament, as the prime minister has an almost unlimited power to appoint people to the House of Lords. Some think the House of Lords is politically irrelevant as its powers to vote down or amend legislation are limited by the Parliament Acts. Yet it has substantial

powers which are only really curbed by convention.
Yes, I am delighted that thanks to the fact that the 216
Conservative peers are outnumbered (and several rarely
support the government), it now defies the government
on an almost daily basis, but it has no mandate, it is
ultimately illegitimate and the government of the day
will always be tempted to bolster the number of loyal
supporters. Moreover, the Lords is already pretty much
the largest legislative body in the world (outnumbered
only by China's National People's Congress) and the
sheer number of new appointments is astounding. In
just over ten years, Tony Blair appointed 374 peers;
in just under three, Gordon Brown added 34. David
Cameron then went into overdrive with 245 new peers
in six years; Theresa May appointed 43 in three years;
and Boris Johnson added another 86 in his three years
(plus seven in his scandalous resignation list). That is
a total of 782 new lords. It's not just the number, it's
the quality of appointees. When Cameron appointed
twenty-six new Conservative peers in August 2015, ten
were former Conservative MPs who had been loyal to
him, one was his deputy chief of staff, two others had
been his head of policy and political secretary, two
were special advisers to Cabinet ministers, four were
Conservative councillors, two others had run in-house
Conservative organisations, and bringing up the rear
was Michelle Mone. This was a cadre of insiders, cronies
and mates, not a serious set of legislators for life. The
Lib Dems, who had just left government and lost most
of their seats, were also rewarded with eleven peers,
including seven ex-MPs, one ex-MEP and the former
chief of staff to Nick Clegg. Labour's list of eight had
seven former MPs. All of which makes me laugh at those
who oppose replacing the Lords with an elected House

on the grounds that it would replicate the Commons. Today's House of Lords already has 173 ex-MPs, many of whom were turfed out by voters.

The power to determine who goes to the Lords is corrupting. The *Sunday Times* has pointed out that anyone who has given the Conservative Party £3 million has become a peer. One such is the billionaire Peter Cruddas, former treasurer of the Conservative Party under David Cameron, who was forced to resign for offering cash for access to potential party donors.[13] Johnson became the first prime minister to overrule the House of Lords Appointments Commission (HOLAC) when it objected to Cruddas' candidacy. But Cruddas is not an exception. The Conservative Party has had forty-four treasurers since 1911; four were already aristocrats; the banker Christopher Holland-Martin MP died in office; Henry Studholme MP was made a baronet; Tim Smith MP was forced to resign over the cash-for-questions scandal; Sir Mick Davis declined a peerage; and Ehud Sheleg has been knighted; but thirty-five, most of whom made substantial political donations, have been given peerages.

I could never persuade Tony Blair to support an elected second chamber with any enthusiasm, but his attempts at reform of the Lords focused on removing the majority of the hereditary peers, cleaning up the appointments process and introducing a degree of transparency so that there was at least some external independent constraint on prime ministerial discretion and utter crooks could be excluded. Hence the creation of HOLAC in 2000. But even this has been undermined in recent years, partly because it has too few powers and has to rely on ministers acting in good faith. Cronyism now abounds. Johnson made Zac Goldsmith a peer and a minister when he lost his Commons seat of Richmond in 2019; and the newly ennobled 'Baron Goldsmith of Richmond Park' let Johnson use his plush Spanish villa for a holiday. Johnson's brother Jo had announced he was retiring from the Commons by saying he could no longer reconcile his family interest with the national interest (as he disagreed so passionately with Boris over Brexit), but he was happy to become 'Baron Johnson of Marylebone' (and, briefly, a minister again). As if to add insult to injury, on his last Friday as prime minister, Johnson appointed Harry Mount as one of the 'independent' members of HOLAC to replace the supposedly independent Charles Moore (whom he had appointed a peer). Mount used to work for Johnson at the *Spectator*, he is a fellow Bullingdon Club member, is the author of the sycophantically titled 192-page tome *The Wit and Wisdom of Boris Johnson* and has been described as Johnson's 'quivering fanboy'. Equally extraordinary was Theresa May's ennoblement of a sitting Labour MP, John Mann, in her resignation honours list in 2019, thereby removing him (albeit with his approval) from a Commons in which no party had a majority. There could be no clearer example of government overreach. And I'm not even going to comment on Boris Johnson's and Liz Truss' resignation honours lists.

I must admit, I have rarely had a constituent write to me about this. A few have sent me their blueprint for reform or abolition of the Lords. But next to none have complained about government's stranglehold on the business and composition of parliament. I understand why. Worries about the cost of living and how to pay the bills feature far more prominently in most people's daily lives. But we should all worry about this, because it's about power – the use and the abuse of power. In the seventeenth century parliament fought against the unfettered power of the Crown. They objected to the monarch's 'personal rule' and the arbitrary abuse of power. Today's substitute for arbitrary monarchy is government with all the power. Parliament needs to rediscover its backbone and reassert its freedom. Good government and better decisions depend on the proper exercise of power. Without it, we are heading towards tyranny.

3

Something Rotten

We were in the prime minister's office behind the Speaker's chair in the Commons: yellow and gold wallpaper by Pugin, a large Arts and Crafts oak table with green leather chairs bearing the crowned portcullis, vast brass chandeliers, linenfold panelling throughout. We were sitting on two green sofas in a more casual corner. Tony Blair had called me in after his latest reshuffle to soften my disappointment at not having been appointed a minister (for the second year in a row). 'The thing is, you're so young, you have your whole life ahead of you. You're still in your twenties,' he said. 'I'm forty-three, Tony,' I replied. He rapidly moved on to other things. 'Which new MPs do you really rate?' he asked. I made a couple of suggestions of Labour colleagues. He looked disappointed. 'The only really impressive one is Chris Huhne,' he said. I didn't know the new Liberal Democrat for Eastleigh, but Tony's remarks were to prove ironic, as Huhne later resigned from the Cabinet, the Privy Council and parliament when he was convicted of perverting the course of justice by persuading his then wife to take his own three speeding points to prevent him from losing his licence. As we parted, Tony had one more piece of advice: 'Just remember, cream always rises to the top.'

I think he meant well, but it didn't really come across that way. Looking at some members of today's front bench, I'm not convinced he was right.

I recount this story because, in essence, politics is about government and government is about what ministers do. As we saw in the last chapter, ministers hold magisterial sway, they act, they take decisions, unlike backbench and Opposition MPs who merely talk and complain about ministers' actions and decisions. So who gets appointed and how they use or abuse the powers granted to them by the monarch on the advice of the prime minister is central to the question of whether and to what extent our system is corrupt (especially when, due to the sheer number of appointments, the PM barely knows half his ministers). That's why this chapter is about capricious ministerial decision-making, abuse of trust and rampant cronyism – and the fact that they are subject to less onerous rules than ordinary MPs. Basically, it's about corruption in government.

Lots of people shrink from the word corruption. You may think it is an exaggeration to say the UK is corrupt, and Alberto Costa, who was a lawyer before he came into parliament as the Conservative MP for South Leicestershire in 2010 and is the longest-standing member of the Standards and Privileges Committees, regularly tells me whenever I bemoan the state of things that 'It's not as if we have *real* corruption in the UK.' That great barrel of moral acuity, Boris Johnson, likewise told the press at COP26 in a strange moment of ladylike protesting too much, 'I genuinely believe that the UK is not remotely a corrupt country and I genuinely think that our institutions are not corrupt.'[1] But I'm far from convinced (not least because I don't trust anyone who says 'genuinely' twice in a sentence), and I have allies. Sir John Major told the BBC in 2022 that Britain is 'politically corrupt';[2] Gordon Brown told LBC that the post-2019 government was the most corrupt 'at least for a century' and that we need 'a new Whitehall and a new Westminster';[3] and, on the back of the government's shenanigans over Owen Paterson, Lord Evans, the chair of the Committee on Standards in Public Life and former director of the Security Service, said that 'we could slip into being a corrupt country'.[4] Robert Barrington, the professor of anti-corruption practices at Sussex University, added that by dismantling or bypassing many of the traditional checks to government power, 'the UK has taken the first steps on a journey towards state capture which ends in being a mid-ranking, politically unstable semi-democracy, with a mid-level economy, in which corruption is prevalent and government is for the purpose of self-perpetuation and not the public interest'.[5]

Some may think this claim of state capture (when narrow interest groups take hold of public policy) is far-fetched, as it is more normally associated with sudden military or authoritarian *coups d'état*, but Barrington argues that the 'incremental subversion of government, which is difficult to see until it has already happened', is even more insidious and that 'the prime danger for the UK is therefore not a single corrupt administration, however undesirable that may be'.[6] He is backed up by the global anti-corruption civil society organisation Transparency International, which reports that the UK has plunged to its lowest ever position in its Corruption Perceptions Index, now ranking 18th. In other words, just when we ought to be aspiring to be the most open, transparent and corruption-free country in the world, a beacon of democracy in a world of increasing autocracy,

I fear we are in danger of sliding down the helter-skelter of shame.

What do I mean by corruption? It can come in many forms. If you asked a Tudor poet, or a theological or moral philosopher of the same period, it involved sexual immorality, licentiousness, fornication, delinquency, adultery, venality or any other form of sinfulness that demonstrated humanity's fallen, corrupted state. Perceptions change, though. For large parts of our history and at least up until the Reform Act in 1832, corruption (including bribing voters, buying and selling government office and seats in parliament, and siphoning off a cut from public funds) was so endemic that it felt like terribly bad luck when someone got caught and had to be made an example of (much like Admiral John Byng, the MP for Rochester, who was executed in 1757, against the wishes of the Commons, as Voltaire put it, *'pour encourager les autres'* – not for corruption but for losing Minorca to France). The fact that many forms of corruption are a thing of the past – and our national assumption that the UK is not fundamentally corrupt – must never blind us to the danger of creeping corruption and the abuse of ministerial discretion.

MINISTERS RULE

Let's briefly go back to the appointment of ministers, because its utter capriciousness is where the rot starts. It is crazily random. My own experience makes the point. I was deputy leader of the House (unpaid) when I received a text from Gordon Brown's foreign policy adviser Tom Fletcher (later ambassador to Lebanon) at 10 a.m. on Monday 8 June 2009. 'Stand by your phone.

Gordon is about to ring you to ask you to be minister for Europe and Latin America.' Great, I thought, my ideal job. Ten minutes later, Tom was on the phone: 'Sorry, Glenys Kinnock rang about something completely different and Gordon has appointed her by accident. What would you like?' 'I could still do Latin America?' I suggested. At 2 p.m. the permanent under-secretary at the Foreign Office, Sir Peter Ricketts, rang to welcome me to the department, but I was moving a Standards and Privileges Report in the Commons, so I only got through to him at 4.45 whereupon he put the ministerial wheels in motion. My new private secretary arrived with a briefing pack just before the Parliamentary Labour Party meeting at 6, after which foreign secretary David Miliband congratulated me and welcomed me to the team. Late that evening I got the call from Gordon. 'I'd like you to go to the Foreign Office,' he said, expecting this to be news to me. 'Great, thanks,' I said. 'You don't sound very surprised,' he said. 'Well, to be honest, I'm already there and my private secretary is briefing me on tomorrow's debate.' Plenty of other ministerial appointments have been just as chaotic. The story goes that during one reshuffle Blair came off the phone and turned to his team. 'Didn't you tell me this person who I've just appointed minister of state for public health was a man?' 'Yes,' they all said, 'he's called Alan Johnson.' 'Well, that was definitely a woman,' he replied. It turned out he had appointed Melanie Johnson – and Alan had to go to Education instead.

The same is true today. Rishi Sunak appointed Suella Braverman as home secretary (five days after she had been sacked for multiple breaches of the Ministerial Code) purely because he had needed her support in the leadership election. Anne-Marie Trevelyan has held six jobs since December 2019, bouncing up and down between minister and secretary of state in different departments (two of which have been abolished or restructured). One feels for those who work in the creative industries, as they've suffered eleven secretaries of state for culture in ten years. What is more, it is rare (if not completely exceptional) for a minister to be appointed because they know something about the subject. If anything, prime ministers fear round pegs in round holes and show little real interest in anyone below Cabinet rank. The only thing that even vaguely approaches a normal appointments process is the perfunctory vetting of potential new ministers by the propriety and ethics team at Downing Street (which failed to spot anything amiss in Sunak's appointments of Nadhim Zahawi, Sir Gavin Williamson or Suella Braverman). That's politics, you might say, but the point is, as often as not it is a complete fluke that someone ends up a minister, especially when the governing party is going through the spin cycle at 1,600 revolutions per second. The Ministerial and other Salaries Act 1975 (one of the most complex and untransparent pieces of legislation on the statute books, but a core part of our constitutional settlement) says the prime minister can appoint 109 paid ministers; and since the House of Commons Disqualification Act 1975 stipulates that no more than 95 can be MPs, the rest are peers. Up to twenty-one can hold one of the highest Cabinet offices as prime minister, chancellor of the Exchequer or secretary of state, and the rest are junior ministers (ministers of state outranking parliamentary under-secretaries of state). That means we have far more ministers than France (41), Australia (42) or India (78). If you add in the forty PPSs and thirteen government MPs who are trade envoys, there are now 148 Conservative MPs on the government payroll, more than 40 per cent of the parliamentary party – which is quite a stranglehold.

An MP's life changes dramatically when they become a minister. They are suddenly bound by the rule of collective responsibility, whereby they must support all government policies and decisions, even if they privately disagree with them. They have to toe the line. And their workday is spent in the department with rarer forays into parliament (where they can only speak for the government on their portfolio). There are so many that the PM cannot possibly know them all – or vouch for their integrity. Which is why I believe we should cut the number of ministers – and make them all properly accountable by requiring them to correct the record when they make a mistake, subjecting them to the same rules as other MPs, putting the Ministerial Code on a statutory basis and closing down their discretion over appointments and government expenditure.

This matters because the public should be able to trust its ministers to be competent, professional and ethical, and always to act in the national or public interest. Yes, people might differ about how best to pursue the national interest, but the central assumption should be that they will always seek the common good, even if it may be to their personal or partisan detriment, because, as Churchill put it, an MP's order of priorities must be country, constituency, party and not the other way round. This indubitably becomes more difficult for ministers who have been in power for a long period. I remember it before the general election in 2010. We looked at the Opposition and dreaded them taking over, so we conflated the national interest with our party's interest. The same is happening today.

Yet the rules for ministers are much less clear or onerous than those for ordinary MPs. Witness the Ministerial Code, which prime ministers have published by convention (not statute) since 1997. It was formerly known as 'Questions of Procedure for Ministers' and goes back to the post-war era. It lays out what is expected of ministers. They must, for instance, declare outside interests (including unremunerated ones) to their departmental permanent secretary. The independent adviser on ministers' interests (a post that has existed since 2006 and is sometimes referred to as the ethics adviser) collates this information and publishes what they think is relevant roughly every six months, along with a report on the code. As the row over Rishi Sunak's registration of interests (and those of his wife) has shown, this is utterly opaque – the very opposite of transparent. Nobody has yet satisfactorily explained to me why this is only published twice a year (and not at all during the several spells when there has been no adviser). The frequency of ministerial sackings and resignations means that the list is rarely an accurate list of ministers, let alone of ministers' interests. You would have thought that it was in the public interest for any interests to be published within days of a minister's appointment, but sometimes a minister's interest is so out of date that the adviser never even publishes it.

But that is not the only flaw in the scheme. The adviser can launch investigations into breaches of the Ministerial Code only with the agreement of the prime minister – which almost by definition means that they cannot investigate the prime minister. It is therefore far from clear what one is to make of a prime minister who knowingly misleads parliament and refuses to correct the record or breaches any other aspect of the Ministerial

Code. Nor can the adviser publish the results of any investigation without the prime minister's permission. Which is why the post is not very independent at all. This was evident when the adviser, Sir Alex Allan, published his report into allegations that the then home secretary Priti Patel had bullied civil servants in several government departments. One was said to have collapsed after a meeting with her, another received a £25,000 pay-off without admission of liability from the department when they claimed Patel had bullied them and the former permanent secretary at the Home Office claimed she had run a 'vicious and orchestrated campaign' against him. Allan concluded 'that the Home Secretary has not consistently met the high standards required by the Ministerial Code of treating her civil servants with consideration and respect. Her approach on occasions has amounted to behaviour that can be described as bullying in terms of the impact felt by individuals. To that extent her behaviour has been in breach of the Ministerial Code, even if unintentionally.'[7] Yet Johnson simultaneously published an alternative contradictory account and announced his decision to keep Patel, prompting Allan's resignation. It gave the all-too-familiar sense that there was one rule for friends of Boris and another for everyone else. Put simply, if she had treated parliamentary staff as it is alleged she treated civil servants, she could well have faced serious repercussions including an ICGS investigation and suspension from the House. Thanks to the culture of ministerial impunity, she got away with it.

The capricious nature of these arrangements is further highlighted by the case of Dominic Raab. Similar allegations had been circulating about him long before Rishi Sunak appointed him justice secretary, but there was no independent adviser in place, so under pressure from the mounting number of complaints, Sunak set up an ad hoc arrangement whereby Adam Tolley KC would investigate and report back. Tolley's terms of reference notably omitted any option for Tolley to decide whether there had been a breach of the Ministerial Code. Although, as Raab pointed out in his resignation letter, the inquiry dismissed all but two of the claims. Raab resigned when Tolley found that he had engaged in an 'abuse or misuse of power' when foreign secretary, and had 'acted in a manner which was intimidating' towards officials at the Ministry of Justice.[8] However, he refused to apologise and sought to portray himself as the victim. Whatever one's personal take on his behaviour, the lack of a permanent, independent body charged with adjudicating whether there has been a breach of the Ministerial Code – and what sanction there should be – is a fundamental flaw.

Johnson's casual approach to the truth – which we will explore further in Chapter 4 – and to matters of ministerial integrity also led to the resignation of Allan's replacement, Christopher (Lord) Geidt. He and I only coincided briefly, but I found Christopher to be a decent, proper, perhaps overly discreet gentleman horrified at being caught in the quicksand of Johnson's turpitude. He ended up having to do terrible contortions to justify not resigning, not least when it was proved that Johnson had lied to him about Lord Brownlow's hefty donation towards the exorbitant costs of refurbishment of the private flat in Downing Street. Geidt's 2022 annual report contained the extraordinary comment that he had avoided giving Johnson unprompted advice about the latter's obligations under the Ministerial Code because if it had been rejected he would have had to resign. He needn't have bothered worrying about it. Five weeks later he was effectively forced out when he was asked to approve what he called a 'deliberate and purposeful breach of the Code'. Quite rightly, he said he would have nothing to do with it.

The lack of independence is borne out by the fact that Transparency International reported in December 2022 that they had found forty potential breaches of the Ministerial Code over the previous five years that had never been investigated by the adviser, either because there was no adviser in post, or because they were blocked by the prime minister, or because the adviser did not think there was enough evidence.[9] Seemingly, the only means an independent adviser has of proving their independence is by resigning. Several bodies including the Institute for Government have called for the Ministerial Code and the adviser to be put on a genuinely independent and statutory footing. As long ago as 2012 Sir Bernard Jenkin called for the code to be 'owned by Parliament and controlled by Parliament in order that it can become a mechanism that can be used by Parliament to hold Ministers to account'. By rejecting the findings against Priti Patel, refusing to initiate investigations into other ministers and testing to destruction the patience of two independent advisers, Johnson brought the whole Ministerial Code system into manifest disrepute, but Sunak still refuses to improve it. I just hope that the new adviser, Sir Laurie Magnus, has plenty of backbone, although I worry that the Ministerial Code system is so opaque that it has already persuaded him that ministers should be allowed considerable privacy when it comes to their outside financial interests.

There is also a double bind for the prime minister when allegations swirl about a minister. One would hope that any PM will want to ensure due process and a fair hearing (although this was not evident under Johnson), but that can take time. Meanwhile the scandal builds until the PM has no choice but to sack his colleague. On the back of allegations about Nadhim Zahawi's tax affairs, the former Tory Party chairman Sir Jake Berry suggested that the PM should be able to suspend a minister as a neutral act pending an inquiry. This makes eminent sense, especially in cases like that of Dominic Raab, who was accused of bullying staff in several departments yet remained in post for months, during which more and more negative stories against him appeared in the media, which Raab understandably sought to rebut. The same has been true of every minister who has faced serious allegations about inappropriate behaviour. With their time taken up or firefighting and protecting their reputation, they are unable to do their job properly.Ministers are entitled to due process, but civil servants are also entitled to a safe workplace. In any other line of work precautionary suspension would be standard practice. Politics shouldn't be the exception.

Current ministers deal with the independent adviser on ministers' interests – and former/sacked/resigned ministers have to do business with the Advisory Committee on Business Appointments (ACOBA), which considers applications about outside jobs for former ministers and senior civil servants. It sounds impressive. In theory at least it is meant to stop ministers (and senior civil servants) from using the privileged information they acquire in post to feather their own nest after leaving office, as they are required to seek permission to take on any work for two years after resigning or being sacked. Sadly, its major flaw is in the first word of its title. It is purely advisory. Consequently, as the Public Administration and Constitutional Affairs

Select Committee has rightly said more than once, it is 'toothless'. Which is why ministers regularly and repeatedly ignore it. One recent example is Nadine Dorries, who took on a role as a presenter on TalkTV without asking permission. ACOBA's rebuke suggests that the risks in being appointed as a broadcaster are usually limited, as the main aim is to prevent individuals from drawing on privileged information or lobbying the government. But Dorries had been the culture secretary with responsibility for broadcasters, including TalkTV. Mostly ACOBA rubber-stamps every application, advising former ministers not to abuse any 'privileged information' they may have, but there is no means of policing this and the two-year cooling off period is too short. The former chancellor Sajid Javid isn't breaking the rules by becoming an adviser to the Jersey-based investment firm Centricus Partners (£300,000 a year). Nor is the former education secretary, Sir Gavin Williamson, who is adviser to RTC Education (£50,000 a year), nor the former justice secretary, Sir Robert Buckland, who is senior counsel for Payne Hicks Beach solicitors (£4,000 a month). Nor is the former culture minister Ed (now Lord) Vaizey, who registers more than two dozen roles as adviser or consultant to cultural and digital organisations. Former ministers are entitled to earn a living, but when, as Transparency International reports, 170 ministers and senior officials have taken roles related to their former policy briefs in the six years between 2017 and 2023, it is difficult not to be concerned that the companies concerned are buying privileged access via Whitehall's revolving door.

What's clear is that ACOBA is patent nonsense. As the Committee on Standards in Public Life has said,

'No system of ethical regulation can sustain the trust of the public, or those it is meant to regulate, when its primary method of enforcement serves only to highlight the lack of any meaningful sanctions for rule-breakers.'[10] Even the ACOBA chair, Eric (Lord) Pickles, says that ministerial contracts should include a provision to allow the government to claw back up to three months' salary for those who refused to follow ACOBA's advice.

There is another flaw in ACOBA. Its standard advice to a former minister who is taking up outside employment is that they may not lobby government on behalf of the company concerned for two years from their last day in ministerial office. This might apply to an ex-minister who also becomes an ex-MP, but it suggests that an ex-minister who remains an MP can lobby government on behalf of a company with whom the MP has an ongoing financial interest. That is paid lobbying and it has been explicitly banned since 1695, as we will explore later.

Ministers' work is also overseen, albeit indirectly, by the Office of the Registrar of Consultant Lobbyists, which was set up by the Transparency of Lobbying, Non-Party Campaigning and Trade Union Administration Act in 2014. It is not a regulator – it can impose no sanction – although failing to register is a criminal offence, but it seeks to bring transparency into the work of consultant lobbyists in their approaches to ministers and civil servants. However, the Act's definition of 'consultant lobbying' is specific. Individuals are engaged in registrable consultant lobbying only if they fulfil three tests: they communicate with a minister of the Crown or permanent secretary about government policy; they do so in return for payment on behalf of a client (i.e. they do not work in-house for a company or charity, but for hire to clients through a consultancy); and they are registered for VAT.

According to the Act, therefore, a non-VAT-registered MP can lobby, but the rules of the House expressly prohibit paid lobbying, whether or not the MP has reached the financial threshold for VAT. Yet again the Paterson case helps make my point. The registrar of consultant lobbyists initially found that Owen Paterson had engaged in 'consultant lobbying', but when Paterson's lawyers proved that he had not been registered for VAT at the time, the registrar had no choice but to conclude that Paterson had not engaged in consultant lobbying activities as defined by law, although it was 'likely' that his communications with ministers 'would otherwise have been registerable if payment had been made to a VAT registered entity'.[11] Yet again, to quote Mr Bumble in *Oliver Twist*, the law is an ass.

The multiplicity of organisations and definitions brings confusion and impunity for bad behaviour. The time has come for a radical overhaul of the law on lobbying, requiring all lobbyists including in-house representatives to register – and ministers and MPs to declare their interactions with them.

GOVERNMENT AS AN OPEN BOOK

Things got very heated in the Commons on 8 December 2022. The so-called levelling-up secretary Michael Gove had just made a statement about reopening a mine in Whitehaven, but the Speaker Sir Lindsay Hoyle was angry. The printed words in the official record, Hansard, don't quite convey his fury. 'The statement I received was the thinnest ever,' he said, 'but the Minister has gone

long. Between that and what the Opposition and I have
been provided with, there is something missing, which
is not in accordance with the ministerial code. We do
not work like that.'[12] In other words, he was directly
accusing the minister of breaching the Ministerial Code
by making a far lengthier statement than he had given
notice of, thereby forcing the shadow minister to reply
to major announcements entirely off the cuff. Quite
exceptionally, the Speaker twice suspended the House
and several of us witnessed him give Gove a dressing
down outside the chamber ('a bollocking' was how one
newspaper reported it).

Why? Put simply, the Ministerial Code expressly
requires ministers to abide by the seven Nolan
Principles of Public Life. Two of these are especially
important when it comes to ministers' interactions with
parliament: accountability and openness. The public
rightly presume that ministers must be accountable
to the public for their decisions and actions and
must submit themselves to the scrutiny necessary to
ensure this. Obviously, the primary expression of that
accountability is through parliament. That is why it has
long been accepted that ministers should confidentially
give due notice (i.e. at least an hour) to their opposite
number of what they are about to say. Anything less
denies the House the ability to scrutinise decisions
properly and is therefore a denial of full accountability.

Even more importantly, however, the Ministerial
Code also states, 'When Parliament is in session, the
most important announcements of Government policy
should be made, in the *first* instance, in Parliament.'[13]
So ministers should act and take decisions in an open
and transparent manner, never withholding information
from the public unless there are clear, necessary and

lawful reasons for doing so. Yet again, the primary place for ministers to demonstrate that openness is in parliament.

Yet some ministers go out of their way to avoid accountability and openness and have repeatedly tested the patience of successive Speakers by briefing – or leaking – details to the press long before they come to the House. In the first half of 2022 alone Speaker Hoyle was forced to reprimand Michael Gove for such a breach on 10 January, Downing Street on 14 January, the Education Department on 1 February, Dominic Raab on 17 March, Nigel Huddleston on 25 April and Dominic Raab again on 22 June. These covered sensitive issues including building safety following the Grenfell Tower fire, police Partygate questionnaires, and plans to curb judicial review and introduce a new Bill of Rights. On the last occasion Hoyle told the House, 'Yet again, the media have been the *first* to know. I am glad the Deputy Prime Minister is making *this* statement, but he should have done so before speaking to the media.'[14]

Even worse has been the apparent disdain for proper accountability shown by chancellors of the Exchequer. There was a time when a chancellor went into purdah for several weeks in advance of any major fiscal statement and any leak of its content was considered a resigning matter. Huw Dalton, for instance, had to stand down as chancellor in 1947 when details of his Budget appeared in an evening newspaper before he told the House. These days, however, Treasury ministers trawl the television studios ahead of the Budget and it's not just snippets of information that appear – it's virtually the whole thing. All the key elements of George Osborne's 2013 Budget appeared in the *Evening Standard* before he delivered them; many speculated that private leaks of Kwasi

Kwarteng's mini-budget of September 2022 enabled billionaire hedge-fund managers to enrich themselves by betting on the pound; and so much of Rishi Sunak's Budget statement in October 2021 had been briefed in advance that the Speaker granted an urgent question the day beforehand, forcing a minister to come to the House to explain himself. Hoyle explained, 'I want the House, and especially the Government, to be clear that if the Government continue to treat this House in this discourteous manner, I will do everything in my power to ensure that Ministers are called here at the earliest opportunity to explain themselves.'[15] As for Jeremy Hunt's 2023 Spring Budget, virtually the only element that had not been pre-announced was the regressive abolition of the £1 million cap on pension pots.

The granting of an urgent question (UQ) is virtually the only power the Speaker has over ministerial accountability, but the fact that the number of UQs has risen dramatically over the years is an indication of how often the Speaker has had to rebuke ministers. It is an imperfect tool, however, as the Speaker has no power to decide *who* will answer for the government, and senior ministers seem to think answering an urgent question is beneath them. When, for instance, Suella Braverman was appointed home secretary for the second time, she sent junior ministers Jeremy Quin and Robert Jenrick to answer for her, even though the questions were about her resignation, reappointment and personal conduct and could fully be answered only by her. That's why the Speaker should be empowered to specify which minister answers a UQ.

One other historic aspect of ministers' accountability to parliament has been the twenty days allocated to motions tabled by the Opposition every session under

Standing Order 14.* Government used to accept that a vote of the House on an Opposition motion might not be legally binding on ministers, but it was morally and politically binding. In consequence it tried to amend and/or vote down every Opposition motion that was critical of government or expressed a wish to change ministerial policy. When Labour was in power, therefore, the Conservatives crafted a host of motions designed to embarrass Labour MPs into voting against their government (including one on post office closures which required MPs in marginal seats to vote for the closure of named Crown post offices in their own constituency). The corollary was that when the government lost a vote, it implemented the vote of the House. The classic example came on 29 April 2009, when a Liberal Democrat motion demanded enhanced settlement rights for Gurkha veterans (a campaign led by the actress Joanna Lumley). The government lost by twenty-one votes – and announced an about-turn the next day. That was accountability in action. However, when Theresa May lost her Commons majority in 2017, she decided not to seek to amend Opposition motions and just let them through without a vote – and then ignored them. Boris Johnson initially took advantage of his majority in 2019 to amend and vote down such motions, but when his new intake of MPs faced fury for voting down footballer Marcus Rashford's call for free school meals during the pandemic, Johnson also started to ignore them. For a while the government conceded that when an Opposition Day motion was passed, the

---

*A parliament runs from its first sitting after a general election until it is dissolved before the next. A parliamentary session starts with the State Opening of Parliament and the King's Speech – and runs until it is prorogued (see p. 50).

relevant minister would respond to the vote by making a statement to the House within a set period. But Jacob Rees-Mogg abandoned this very limited concession in January 2021. This deliberate abandonment of a traditional means of holding government (and its supporters) to account undermines parliamentary accountability. It turns Opposition Days into little more than fireside debates and renders the Commons as obsolete as a dodo's appendix. Conservatives may admire such legal insouciance now, but they would despair if Labour were to adopt the same strategy in government.

There is one (arcane) exception. According to Erskine May, both Houses have long had 'the power to call for the production of papers by means of a motion for a return … by means of an humble address to the sovereign'.[16] In practice that means the Commons passes a motion addressed to the King demanding the production of papers – which the King's ministers can't refuse. Since such motions are binding, Labour started using this device in November 2017 and has done so on fifteen further occasions, on nine of which the government has not opposed the motion and has subsequently (albeit slowly) abided by the ruling of the House. Sadly, it's the exception that proves the rule that ministers nowadays regularly and imperiously ignore parliament, partly because there is no means of enforcing their adherence to the Nolan Principles.

SUNLIGHT — THE BEST DISINFECTANT

Ministers have the same attitude to openness. The House of Commons Code of Conduct requires MPs to register all outside financial interests within twenty-eight days, including employment, travel, gifts and hospitality over the value of £300. This means that if you and your partner attend a dinner worth £151 each, you have to register the details of the cost and who paid for it. Or for instance if you go to the Brit Awards (cost c. £900) or Glastonbury (c. £660) courtesy of UK Music, you have to register it and you are barred for twelve months[*] from approaching ministers or officials, or taking part in a proceeding in parliament with the aim of seeking a material benefit for UK Music. This rule used to apply to all MPs, without distinction.[17] Since 2015, however, the Code has allowed an exemption for ministers acting 'in their ministerial capacity'. The argument is that their outside financial interests will appear in their department's 'transparency returns', which separately detail travel, gifts, hospitality and meetings and are published on the government's website quarterly. This means that if two MPs are taken to an expensive football match together and are wined and dined by a commercial client, the backbench MP will have to declare the hospitality within twenty-eight days if it costs more than £300 – and will have to provide full details of the client and the cost. But a government minister will be able to claim that they only attended in a ministerial capacity – and the public will only know limited details about it several months later. This is plainly barmy, not least as ministers make decisions and the public has the right to know what might be influencing those decisions.

Under these preposterous rules, Priti Patel claimed that she had been given free tickets to the premiere of *No Time to Die* by the Jamaican Tourist Board in her 'ministerial capacity' as home secretary and when

---

[*]It was for six months until we changed the rule on 1 March 2023.

I questioned ministers Mark Spencer and Michael Ellis about this at the Standards Committee in 2022, Ellis said she had attended because 'The nature of the film, one could argue, is connected to executive functions.'[18] In other words, she went because James Bond is a spy and she is in charge of spies. Leaving aside the fact that Bond (who is a fictional character) works for MI6, which is the responsibility of the foreign secretary not the home secretary, it is that kind of argument that makes ministers look ridiculously shabby. This anomaly is also exposed by Boris Johnson's family holiday to Spain in October 2021, when he used the VIP 'Windsor' suite at Heathrow (courtesy of the airport, value £1,800) and stayed for free at Zac Goldsmith's luxurious property near Marbella. He declared the former with the House authorities but decided that the latter was given in his 'ministerial capacity' and therefore did not attribute a value to the free hospitality when it was published in the register of ministerial interests. This is clearly nonsensical. (Equally inexplicable is the fact that the Cabinet secretary and the propriety and ethics team in the Cabinet Office decided that it was absolutely fine for Johnson to enjoy an £800,000 credit facility while he was in Downing Street, guaranteed by a Canadian millionaire, Sam Blyth, and for this to be kept secret because they did not deem it 'relevant' for disclosure, by virtue of Blyth being a family member.[19] How they arrived at such a decision, when Blyth is so distant a cousin that Johnson had never met him until they were introduced by the Tory donor Richard Sharp is impossible to fathom.) The Lords, who, like the Commons, govern themselves, have much less onerous registration rules. The threshold for declaration is higher and they don't declare the actual amount of benefit in cash or in kind they have received. Peers don't receive a salary, but one day someone will wake up to the fact that their House exercises considerable power yet faces negligible scrutiny.

The Standards Committee has recommended that the ministerial-capacity exemption be abolished, but sadly the government held out against this when the Commons agreed the Committee's new Code of Conduct in December 2022. I was perplexed by the government's objection, especially when Penny Mordaunt claimed that ministers could not possibly register their outside financial interests with the House by 1 March 2023, as it worryingly implies that they don't know what their outside interests are. But at least she guaranteed 'monthly reporting' of ministers' interests and a full alignment with the Commons register of interests 'by the start of the summer'.[20] She even specified 2023. What still worries me is that there is no means of investigating whether a minister has fully declared and registered their financial interests and ministers think they are exempt from declaring relevant interests in parliament.

As the Nolan definition of openness makes clear, ministers should never withhold information from the public 'unless there are clear and lawful reasons for so doing'. Two interconnected instances will suffice to make the point that government is failing in this regard. First, the Russia Report, which was produced in 2019 by the Intelligence and Security Committee.[*] It concluded that there had been serious attempts by the Russian state to undermine and influence the British democratic system. Because the Committee is appointed by the

---

[*]The ISC is an unusual Commons committee in that it consists of senior MPs from across the House who are appointed by the prime minister. Departmental select committees by contrast are appointed by the House on the basis of elections in each of the parties and the chairs are elected by the whole House.

prime minister, who is able to control its publications, Boris Johnson delayed its publication until after the election (and even then only in an abbreviated and redacted version). I suspect he did so because he feared that people would conclude that Russia had sought to influence the EU referendum. Interestingly, when asked whether he had ever seen evidence of any such interference, both he and Theresa May stated that they had not seen 'any *successful* attempts' to undermine the democratic processes in several countries, but declined to say they were successful.[21]

Secondly, Tier 1 or 'golden' visas. From 2008 to 2022 the UK offered 'Tier 1 investor' visas to foreign citizens with large amounts of money to invest. Those with £2 million were entitled to indefinite leave to remain after five years, those with £10 million could apply after just two. Some of us worried from the outset that this VIP visa route was open to abuse by people who had acquired their wealth illegitimately or were involved in wider corruption, as no checks were made on the source of applicants' funds, and up until 2015 applicants did not even have to have a UK bank account. In addition, Transparency International reported in 2015 that it was likely that the scheme had been used to launder 'substantial amounts of corrupt wealth' from Russia and China. The Foreign Affairs Select Committee expressed concern about these visas in its report on Russian corruption in 2018, which is when the government launched a retrospective review of successful individual applicants up to 2015. This eventually led the home secretary Priti Patel to close this route in February 2022. She promised to publish the review 'soon' but it did not see the light of day until January 2023 – and the version that eventually appeared under Suella Braverman consisted solely of edited highlights. These included the shocking revelation that a 'small minority of individuals' who got a UK golden visa were at high risk of having obtained their wealth through corruption or illicit finance or organised crime, and that 'the route attracted a disproportionate number of applicants from the countries identified in the UK's National Risk Assessment of money laundering and terrorist financing 2020'.[22] Amazingly, the government also admitted that ten golden visa recipients were subsequently sanctioned Russian oligarchs – which prompts the question of why we were inviting people with evidently disreputable sources of funds to base themselves in the UK. Despite these very belated revelations, the government omitted all the relevant details, including how many individuals who had been granted Tier 1 visas were found to be at high risk of corruption or organised crime, which countries they came from, how many of these high-risk individuals were granted or refused indefinite leave to remain or British citizenship, how many have subsequently been sanctioned and any analysis of the 5,435 golden visas issued from 2015 to 2023. Moreover, when Dame Margaret Hodge and Layla Moran have tried to elicit further details the minister, Tom Tugendhat, has responded with 'we will not be commenting further'. Yet again, this is a manifest failure to be open and transparent.

Why does this matter? Partly because the public are entitled to know whether the 'golden visa' scheme seriously impacted national security – and if so, why it was continued for so long. On top of that it is perfectly possible that some Russians who have been granted British citizenship have been encouraged either subsequently or simultaneously to give money to the Conservative Party. Thus Vladimir Chernukhin, who was Russia's deputy finance minister from 2000 to 2002 and then chairman of a state bank, fled to the UK when he was sacked by Putin in 2004 and became a British citizen in 2011. He married Russian-born British resident Lubov Golubeva in 2007. She started donating to the Conservative Party in 2012, becoming the biggest political donor in British history, giving more than £2.1 million. Both husband and wife claim to have no connections with Putin. Yet the BBC revealed in September 2020 that Mr Chernukhin had secretly received $8 million in 2016 from the billionaire Suleiman Kerimov[23] who is a member of the upper house of the Russian parliament and is now sanctioned by the UK, the EU and the US as a close Putin ally. The BBC also revealed in April 2022 that Mrs Chernukhin had been a director of a UK-based company linked to Kerimov in 2006.[24] Mrs Chernukhin's lawyers have said that she 'has never received money deriving from Mr Kerimov or any company related to him' and her 'donations to the Conservative Party have never been tainted by Kremlin or any other influence'.[25] However, it is difficult not to agree with *The Times* columnist Edward Lucas who concluded that 'the Chernukhins, pleasant people that they might be ... are not fit and proper people to make donations to a British political party'.[26] The Conservative Party asserts that it has always abided by the law in relation to such donations. But it must surely be time to place a legal requirement on British political parties to do due diligence to identify the true source of donations and thereby better protect our democracy from potentially criminal funds.

One final point about openness. This book is about parliament, but the media are also one of the cornerstones of democracy. They need unfettered access to do their work. We should be scandalised when political parties (and especially the government of the day) restrict attendance at their events to favourable media outlets or favoured journalists. Client journalism is the bane of British politics, but it only prospers because politicians enable it.

FAVOURITISM, NEPOTISM AND CLIENTELISM

By virtue of the government's parliamentary majority alone, ministers also exercise power in appointing people to public bodies. The Ministerial Code and the Nolan Principles require that such powers should be exercised without partiality of any kind. Yet this is another rule that seems to be constantly ignored.

Formally speaking, nepotism means appointing your nephew (in Latin *nepos*) to a lucrative post, but it now refers to any form of advantage, privilege or position that is awarded to a family member, friend or associate. For a long time, though, nepotism was considered common sense. When, for instance, the deputy of the home secretary Viscount Melbourne died in 1833, the prime minister Earl Grey immediately recommended that his own son, Viscount Howick, take the post. Melbourne's only objection was that Howick might be too squeamish about imposing the death penalty. Likewise, the Conservative prime minister 'Bob' Cecil, the 3rd Marquess of Salisbury, appointed his son Viscount Cranborne and two nephews, Arthur and Gerald Balfour, as ministers – and ensured that Arthur Balfour took over when he resigned in 1902.[*]

---

[*]Some have claimed that this is where the phrase 'Bob's your uncle' stems from, but that doesn't explain the longer version, 'Bob's your uncle and Fanny's your aunt', nor the fact that it only became popular after a music revue in the 1920s.

Such favouritism is alive and well in UK politics. Witness Rachel Johnson interviewing Stanley Johnson about Boris Johnson, which prompted the Conservative MP Huw Merriman to comment on Twitter, 'when I was a baby, Johnson and Johnson used to powder backsides rather than be paid to talk out of them. There is too much nepotism in politics. It must stop. People must believe they can succeed by merit and hard-work.' Equally incestuous, for that matter, is Nadine Dorries interviewing Boris Johnson on TalkTV or Jeremy Hunt giving a post-Budget 'exclusive' to two fellow Tories on GB News, the husband-and-wife team, Philip Davies and Esther McVey. The list of Tory MPs with regular programmes is now so long it is likely to bring public service broadcasting into disrepute.

There has also been a steady but perceptible politicisation of the honours system, which grants honorific awards like OBEs and knighthoods (as opposed to the system for putting people in the Lords). Sir Vernon Ellis told Channel 4 that when he, as chair of the Cabinet Office's Arts and Media Honours Committee between 2012 and 2015, complained that giving an honour to a particular Tory donor 'would bring the honours into a bit of disrepute', he was told to be 'pragmatic' and his own appointment was not renewed. Likewise, Louise Casey, who chairs the Community and Voluntary Service Honours Committee, wrote to the Cabinet Office to complain, saying, 'It's no secret I've struggled with the politicalisation [sic] of the honours and especially with the last incumbents of No 10 ... I know balancing a demanding No 10 with many other pressures is hard, but I also owe it to myself to say when I think something is not right.' And Waheed Saleem, who sat on the same committee (but was not renewed after three years), has claimed that, when they rejected some nominations, Downing Street submitted them again until they got the 'right answer'.[27]

Another pleasant bauble with which to tempt party donors is a seat on one of the prestigious national arts organisations. The chair of the BBC is a classic instance. There are rare exceptions – Tony Blair, for instance, in 2004 appointed as chair Michael Grade who later became a Conservative peer – but the tendency on both sides has been for the prime minister of the day to appoint a political supporter. Hence Charles Hill, George Howard, Marmaduke Hussey, Christopher Bland, Gavyn Davies, Chris Patten and Rona Fairhead. Then there is the last incumbent Richard Sharp, who has donated more than £400,000 to the Conservative Party and introduced Boris Johnson to Boris' distant cousin Sam Blyth just before Boris appointed him to the BBC. The same applies across a swathe of arts organisations, despite the fact that they are all meant to be politically neutral. The Conservative Party are not shy about this. They claim it is fair play. As an email from Conservative Campaign HQ to party donors put it in 2019, 'It is important Conservatives rebalance the representation at the head of these important public bodies.'[28] Of course, it might just be a coincidence and perhaps these appointees bring something special to the table, but John Booth gave £207,000 in 2017 and was made a trustee of the National Gallery in August 2021 (and chair of the committee that awards honours in the arts and media in 2022); Howard Shore has given £1.75 million and is now a trustee of the Tate; David Ross, who provided Johnson with a holiday home in Mustique and has given more than £1 million, is chair of the National Portrait Gallery (along with Chris Grayling MP); Lord Marland, a Tory

peer who has donated more than £300,000 to the party, is
a trustee of the British Museum; James Lambert, whose
firm has donated more than £80,000 to the party, is a
trustee of the National Gallery; as is Dounia Nadar, who
has donated more than £66,000. Given Conservatives'
apparent determination to appoint their preferred
loyalty-checked candidates, I almost feel sorry for Paul
Dacre whom they twice failed to get appointed to chair
Ofcom, perhaps because he knew absolutely nothing
about broadcasting.

When they run out of arts bodies, there are always
non-executive appointments in government departments
to consider. They may be less glamorous, but they are
more influential. Fortunately for the government, the
person who oversees these is Lord Nash, a Tory peer
who, with his wife, has contributed more than £500,000
to the Conservative Party. Dominic Johnson, the chief
executive of Somerset Capital Management, a firm
co-founded by Jacob Rees-Mogg, has done well out of his
connection. He was a non-executive at the Department
for International Trade and is now a peer and minister in
the same department. Likewise, the financier and donor
Ben Goldsmith was a non-executive director at the
Department for Environment, Food and Rural Affairs,
where his elder brother was a minister; and Ranjit Baxi,
the co-chairman of the Conservative Friends of India,
who is a businessman in the recycling industry, is a non-
executive director at the Department for Transport.
None of these party affiliations is included on the
government websites that record these appointments.
There is no law or rule that requires it, but transparency
should surely be the order of the order.

You might argue that this has little to do with
parliament, but ministerial authority stems from

parliament and it is high time that the responsibility for these appointments was transferred to parliament as a whole so that their openness and transparency can be guaranteed.

ABUSE OF DISCRETION

Another Nolan Principle is objectivity, the idea that 'Holders of public office must act and take decisions impartially, fairly and on merit, using the best evidence and without discrimination or bias.'[29] The polar opposite of this is perhaps the most common form of corruption around the world, where the discretion vested in an individual is abused for personal gain. A police officer deliberately stops a driver for a minor traffic infringement and agrees to let them off in exchange for a fine, which he pockets. A planning officer waves a development through in exchange for a kickback. Transparency International's definition of this abuse is concise: 'abuse of entrusted power for private gain'.[30] But speaking for the government, Lord Sharpe told the Lords that it went much further. 'Corruption,' he said, 'is the abuse of entrusted power for private benefit that usually breaches laws, regulations, standards of integrity and/or standards of professional behaviour. Corruption need not be economic in nature and can still exist even if everyone has acted within the law.'[31]

The evidence suggests this is rare in the UK. It is a long time since we had a flagrant scandal of this kind – although most MPs and councillors will have had someone at some point allege that the reason they've not been allowed to extend their house is because of 'corruption in the council'. To which I always say, 'Report it to the police.'

However, two things have made my blood boil. First is the awarding of PPE contracts by ministers during the pandemic. Don't get me wrong. I know everyone was desperate to protect NHS and care home staff. We all thought government should do everything in its power to get hold of the equipment as fast as possible (although we might also have asked why we weren't ready for this in advance). Speed was of the essence, corners might have to be cut and normal procurement rules requiring open competition and tendering might have to be relaxed. The question is, were too many corners cut and were they cut in a way that was reckless, discriminatory and corrupt? Ministers say not. Julia Lopez, then a junior minister at the Cabinet Office, told the Commons in March 2021 that 'there have been no corners cut'.[32] But this flies in the face of the evidence, as both the courts and the National Audit Office have shown.

At the heart of the problem was the 'VIP lane', through which government members and supporters could recommend companies for PPE and other Covid contracts worth many millions of pounds. Ministers say that the VIP lane did not make a material difference, as all bids had to be judged on their eventual merits by civil servants, who 'did not rely on referral to the high priority lane when awarding contracts'.[33] But according to the National Audit Office, £10.5 billion of contracts were awarded between March and July 2020 without any competitive process. Mrs Justice O'Farrell ruled in the High Court that the system was unlawful and that 'Offers that were introduced through the senior referrers received earlier consideration at the outset of the process. The high priority lane team was better resourced and able to respond to such offers on the same day that they arrived, in contrast to the opportunities team (which assessed suppliers and their offers not prioritised through the VIP lane), where the sheer volume of offers prevented such swift consideration.'[34] The government claimed that it was highly likely that these same offers would have been awarded without going through the VIP lane, but this is the definition of preferential treatment. And it worked. According to the National Audit Office, companies which bid via this lane were ten times more likely to win a contract than others. Nearly 500 companies with links to ministers or officials were advanced through this lane, 144 were promoted by ministers' private offices and 64 by MPs or peers. Meller Designs, which was co-owned by David Meller, who had backed Michael Gove's bid for leader and donated £60,000 to the Conservative Party, was referred by Gove and won £164 million in Covid contracts.[35] Gove's spokesman denied that the referral involved any impropriety. Liz Truss' adviser at the Board of Trade, Andrew Mills, who was also a senior adviser for Ayanda Capital (which seems a conflict of interest in itself), helped secure £252 million of contracts for the company after officials reportedly marked the referral 'VERY URGENT VIP ESCALATION'. One official wrote that, if the deal fell through, 'Andrew will escalate as high as he can possibly go!' The head of Ayanda, Tim Horlick, told ITV News, 'There was no cronyism involved in the award of the contract. It went through a proper procurement process.'[36] Alex Bourne, a former publican and friend and neighbour of Matt Hancock, sent the health secretary a WhatsApp message and ended up with £50 million of government work supplying vials for the test-and-trace programme. He

told the BBC, 'I know I've done nothing wrong.'[37] Greg
Hands passed on a recommendation from the chair of
a neighbouring Conservative Constituency Association,
Mark Higton, which led to Luxe Lifestyle, a company
with no published accounts at the time and no history
of providing PPE, getting a £25.8 million contract.
A spokesman for Hands said that all he had done was
forward 'a message from someone who contacted him
to the relevant officials'.[38] Strangely, only Conservative
MPs and peers were made aware of the 'VIP lane' – yet
more evidence of the partiality with which the contracts
were awarded.

Even more worryingly, as Spotlight on Corruption
has highlighted, '25 of the 50 companies in the
government's "VIP lane" supplied PPE worth £1 billion
that was not fit for purpose. This amounts to 59% of all
money awarded to VIP lane companies for PPE.'[39] In
other words, some of the contractors recommended by
government insiders were much more likely to succeed –
and much more likely to provide unsuitable equipment.

One other aspect of this is disturbing – ministers'
reluctance to publish details. The Good Law Project, the
law courts and the Commons had to drag the details out
of government. For instance, ministers said in February
2021 that all previous contracts had been published. Boris
Johnson even told the Commons on 22 February that
the contracts were 'on the record for everyone to see'.[40]
But three days later government lawyers admitted that a
further one hundred contracts had to be published and
in June that year they admitted to forty more worth £4.2
billion. The Opposition has twice used its Opposition Day
for humble address motions demanding the publication
of Covid contracts – and on both occasions government
whips have instructed all Conservative MPs to abstain.

In the first case it took months to supply the relevant documents. And in the second the minister has already declared that the response will be delayed and redacted.

Most disturbing of all has been the role of Michelle Mone, who was appointed to the Lords by David Cameron in 2015. She too is said to have recommended a company (which had only just been set up), PPE Medpro, and reportedly aggressively and successfully lobbied Michael Gove and the Cabinet Office minister Lord Agnew on its behalf. She has denied that she had any personal financial interest in the company, and says that is why she has never included it in her register of financial interests, but according to the *Guardian* tens of millions of pounds of PPE Medpro's profits were transferred to an offshore trust of which Mone and her adult children were the beneficiaries. A lawyer speaking on her and her husband's behalf has stated 'there is much inaccuracy in the portrayal of the alleged "facts" and a number of them are completely wrong'.[41] Since these stories broke, the government has announced it is suing PPE Medpro for the £122 million it paid for allegedly faulty sterile surgical gowns, and both the police and the National Crime Agency are said to be investigating potential fraud at the company. Medpro has denied the claims in the defence filed in response to the government's High Court proceedings, stating that they 'performed and executed the Contract as required' and that 'all allegations of breach are misconceived and are in any event denied'. Mone took 'leave of absence' from the Lords on 6 December 2022, but this would not affect any investigation by the Lords standards commissioner and the Conduct Committee, as the *Companion to the Standing Orders and Guide to the Proceedings of the House* (the Lords rulebook) states,

'The House may however refuse or end leave of absence on the application of the Commissioner for Standards or the Conduct Committee, where this is necessary either to enable the Commissioner to conduct an investigation under the Code of Conduct, or to enable the Conduct Committee to impose or recommend the imposition of a sanction on a member.'[42] In other words, the House of Lords may yet revoke her 'leave of absence' and suspend or expel her if it finds she has breached its rules.

THE POLITICS OF THE PORK BARREL

My second concern lies with the number of government 'funds' that have proliferated in recent years where MPs and local authorities have to compete with one another in lobbying ministers for cash.

Let's start with the Towns Fund, which was set up in 2018 and has now allocated £3.6 billion, 'as part of the government's plan to level up our regions'.[43] The allocation process went through two stages. Civil servants did an initial assessment, scoring all English towns against a series of criteria for poverty and under-investment and rating them as high, medium or low priority. Ministers then decided where the money was going. You might have thought that that would mean the funds would go to the highest-priority and therefore poorest towns in the land, but that's not how it worked out. Of the forty-five successful bids announced in the 2021 Budget, only seventeen went to 'high priority' towns, while twenty-eight went to 'medium priority' towns and 79 per cent went to towns in Conservative-held constituencies. The Public Accounts Committee has a Conservative majority, but it said that it was 'not convinced by the rationales for selecting some towns and not others', which were 'vague and based on sweeping assumptions'. It also made the damning point that 'in some cases, towns were chosen by ministers despite being identified by officials as the very lowest priority (for example, one town selected ranked 535th out of 541 towns)'. It concluded that the evident lack of transparency had understandably fuelled accusations of political bias.[44]

You could argue that the whole scheme was rigged from the start. I know from the Rhondda that many towns have suffered a harsh decline over the decades and are in need of investment, but 'towns' is a very specific category. It excludes the poorest inner-city areas of the country and it is tempting to conclude that the real aim behind the fund was to syphon money to Brexit-voting seats with Conservative MPs, especially as decisions were made by ministers. Perhaps the most disturbing aspect of the whole process, however, was that the secretary of state, Robert Jenrick, the MP for Newark, signed off £25 million for Darwen; and the junior minister Jake Berry, the MP for Rossendale and Darwen, signed off £25 million for Newark. They both claim that this was to prevent any imputation of impropriety, but it is difficult not to suspect that this was a ministerial slush fund in all but name. The fact that Rishi Sunak boasted to a group of Conservative Party members in Tunbridge Wells that he had changed funding formulas to divert money from 'deprived urban areas' has added to that sense.

Then there's the £4.8 billion Levelling Up Fund, which is designed to 'support town centre and high street regeneration, local transport projects, and cultural and heritage assets'.[45] Leaving aside the fact that this fund nowhere near matches the cuts to local government since 2010, this is ostensibly a good idea. The UK is riven by regional inequality. But this too seems to be skewed. In the first round of bids, sixty-one out of the hundred poorest areas received no funding and in the 2021–2 financial year, the south-east of England (excluding London), which is the most affluent region in the UK, received £9.2 million, while the north-east, which is the poorest, received just £4.9 million. Ashford in Kent (MP Damian Green) got £14.8 million for a new international film studio and Bedfordshire Council (MP Nadine Dorries) got £6.8 million for a roundabout. The government says that 'bids were assessed by processes that are transparent, robust and fair – and took no account of areas' political control'. But yet again the Public Accounts Committee has not been impressed. It complained in 2022 that 'principles for awarding funding were only finalised by Ministers after they knew who, from the 170 shortlisted bidders, would win and who would not as a result of those principles'.[46] In other words, it was rigged towards ministers' preferred outcomes. The Committee had a simple proposal, namely that the principles for awarding funding should be determined before the names of shortlisted areas are revealed to ministers. You would have thought this was blindingly obvious – but ministers still insist on seeing who is up for funding before they decide the criteria. Since each bid has to be supported by the local MP, this means ministers know which parliamentary colleague is seeking support for their community. I cannot imagine a system more open to abuse. It invites MPs to lobby ministers secretly and encourages ministers to reward favoured party colleagues. It also gives party managers and whips a powerful hold over difficult colleagues, as the once-Conservative-now-Labour MP Christian Wakeford discovered when he threatened to rebel in a Commons vote. He told the BBC, 'I was threatened that I would not get a school for Radcliffe if I didn't vote one particular way. This is a town that's not had a high school for the best part of 10 years. How would you feel holding back the rejuvenation of a town for a vote? It didn't sit comfortably.'[47] He was not alone. His former colleague William Wragg, the chair of the Public Administration and Constitutional Affairs Committee, reported attempts to bully MPs into opposing a motion of no-confidence in Boris Johnson and condemned ministers or whips 'threatening to withdraw investments from members of parliament's constituencies which are funded from the public purse'.[48] (Likewise, WhatsApp messages suggest that Matt Hancock and his special adviser agreed a plan to force a Conservative colleague, James Daly, to vote for new lockdown measures by threatening to deny him a new disabled health hub for his constituency. Matt Hancock's team have denied that the threat was made. Offering or refusing taxpayers' money to persuade constituency MPs how to vote is corrupt. Bizarrely, there is no rule against it. But there should be.)

The second round of awards was no better, as Sunak's constituency of Richmond in Yorkshire, one of the wealthiest in the land, received £19 million. In America they call this 'pork-barrel'. In the UK it smacks of corruption. Discretionary funds are dangerous – and large discretionary funds are even more dangerous. They tempt the government and the member into corruption. And if we really want to tackle economic inequality, funding should not be discretionary or competitive, it should be based on objective criteria and it should be awarded blind. Levelling up should mean, 'From each according to their ability, to each according to their need.' This rapid increase in 'discretionary' funds – which is largely the brainchild of Rishi Sunak – infuriates me and I am shocked that civil servants have been so captured that they have not objected to it.

I started the previous chapter with the drains in Westminster. No city works without fully functioning sewers and our political system is no different. It's always best to flush things out the moment things start to smell a bit iffy and long before things start backing up. I hope that this chapter has shown how dangerous this present moment is, with ministers abusing their considerable powers, failing to live up to the principles of accountability, objectivity and openness and consequently risking an irremediable loss of public trust. To put it plainly, a culture of impunity has taken hold of government. The rules are weaker for ministers than for other MPs – and such as they are, they are rarely enforced with any seriousness. Ministers see their fellows (especially their most senior colleagues) exploit the lack of checks and balances and conclude there is little point in abiding by the letter and the spirit of the rules, let alone the conventions that have never been written down. One discretionary fund breeds another. One dodgy appointment leads to another. As I have said before, blight spreads.

But this is not just about the structural inadequacies of our parliamentary system of ministerial government. It's also about individuals' misconduct. Every instance of lying, abusing your position as an MP and confusing your private interest for the public interest adds to that sense of a parliament mired in sleaze. That is why the next three chapters will focus on areas of manifest failings by individual MPs – the misconduct that so regularly brings the whole House into disrepute.

4

The Worst Lies in London*

Thursday 21 April 2022. The Commons was unusually full for a Thursday. Keir Starmer had written to the Speaker to ask him to allow a debate on a motion to refer Boris Johnson to the Committee of Privileges for lying to parliament. Of course, the motion was dressed up in what we quaintly call 'parliamentary language' (as explained on p. 126). It didn't use anything so vulgar as the word 'lie'. Instead, it suggested that what Johnson had told the House about parties in Downing Street during Covid lockdowns 'appear to amount to misleading the House'. Yet it was specific about the instances when Johnson had misled the Commons. He had said at PMQs on 1 December 2021 that 'all guidance was followed completely in No. 10'; and a week later he doubled down three times, saying that he had been 'repeatedly assured since these allegations emerged that there was no party and that no Covid rules were broken'; he had added, 'I am sickened myself and furious about that, but I repeat what I have said to him [Keir Starmer]: I have been repeatedly assured that the rules were not

---

*With apologies to Stephen Sondheim's song from *Sweeney Todd*, 'The Worst Pies in London'.

broken'; and he had finished with 'the guidance was followed and the rules were followed at all times'.[1]

MPs love to call things 'historic', but that Thursday afternoon certainly was an exceptional moment. No sitting prime minister had ever been referred to the Committee of Privileges for lying to parliament. I was in a strange position. Ever since the old Committee on Standards and Privileges had been split in two with the fourteen-member Standards Committee considering alleged breaches of the Code of Conduct and the seven-member Privileges Committee looking at matters of privilege and contempt of parliament referred to it by the whole House, the working assumption was that both committees had the same chair. I had chaired both since spring 2020 and although most of the workload involved Standards, I had overseen an important Privileges report on what to do with witnesses who refuse to appear before a committee of the House. Inevitably, journalists ask me to comment on every new scandal that hoves into sight, but I have always been scrupulous about not commenting on anything that could possibly come before my Committee, because we exercise a quasi-judicial function and the chair has to be impartial and be seen to be impartial. In the Paterson case, for instance, I had refused to read the newspaper accounts until the commissioner's memorandum appeared before us. And when the commissioner found that Boris Johnson had breached the rules over his free holiday in Mustique, I chaired the meetings that found that, although he had been careless, he had not breached the rules.

But never in a month of Sundays did I think that the House would refer Johnson to Privileges. He enjoyed an eighty-seat majority. Why would a Conservative Commons vote for a Conservative prime minister to be referred to Privileges, unless they had already decided he was a wrong 'un and needed to go? I had consequently held forth on radio, television and in print on what I thought of the matter. It seemed obvious to me that he had lied. He was physically present at some of the 'meetings'. There were photos. He had been fined by the police for attending two. And he had a track record. He had been sacked twice for lying – first by *The Times* for making up a quote in an article and later by Tory leader Michael Howard for falsely denying that he had had an affair with a fellow journalist at the *Spectator*, Petronella Wyatt. And every week seemed to bring a new Johnson lie, half-truth, elision or gross exaggeration.

That's why I was taken aback when I heard that Starmer was thinking of tabling a Privileges motion (in part because the other opposition parties were intending to do the same). I wrote in my diary, 'it's a nonsense. The Committee of Privileges has 4 Tories, three of whom are PPSs. So the likelihood of its achieving anything meaningful is minimal.' But Starmer went ahead and on Tuesday afternoon the Speaker announced there would be a vote on Thursday afternoon. This put me in a quandary. I persuaded myself that I could chair an inquiry impartially because the question was not whether Johnson had lied, but whether he did so knowingly, or recklessly, whether he bothered to check his facts and correct the record and whether his actions amounted to a culpable contempt of parliament. But that was dancing on the head of a pin. More importantly, Tories started complaining. Jacob Rees-Mogg went on air to say that it was nonsense to refer Johnson to a committee chaired by me, whips started briefing against me, the Tory comms team republished my tweets attacking Johnson, and a senior Tory told me that at the 1922 Committee of backbench Tory MPs Johnson had condemned the 'Bryant Committee' as a kangaroo court. Then Sir Graham Brady, the chair of the 1922 Committee, asked for a chat. Would I recuse myself? Yes, if that meant he would support the motion. 'Yes, definitely.' So, on Wednesday morning I announced I was stepping aside from the Privileges Committee. The mood was angry at PMQs. Starmer riled Johnson, who lost his temper. It was clear they hated each other. But that afternoon we had twelve votes in a row, which meant MPs were stuck in the building, chatting, plotting and gossiping for more than two and a half hours. The mood darkened during the votes, as several Tories sidled up to congratulate me. One notoriously robust 'red wall' Tory MP said he was going to have Covid on Thursday (and would therefore not turn up to vote for Johnson). A leading Brexiteer told me he wasn't going anywhere near it. Sir Iain Duncan Smith said he was sure someone thought they had a cunning plan. Another Tory told me that 'Victoria' (either Prentis or Atkins, it wasn't clear) had a list of forty-one Tories who refused to back Boris.

Just as with the Paterson debate, the government tried some last-minute procedural jiggery-pokery. At 8 p.m. – in the middle of the votes – it published an amendment to the main motion, which would postpone a decision on referring Johnson until after the police and Sue Gray had completed their work. It was feeble but it pleased nobody. Dozens of Tories made it clear privately that they'd already been scorched in the Paterson debacle and they were not going to fall for that trick again. At best they would abstain.

After the votes, I slept badly and when I turned up at the Commons on Thursday I presumed we would lose. Dr Andrew Murrison – and another Tory MP who went on to become a minister under Sunak – told me it was all too soon. But that suddenly changed halfway through Business Questions. I wrote in my diary, 'Chris Heaton-Harris (the Tory chief whip) sidled up to Jacob Young, the 2019 MP for Redcar who looks as if he's so over-excited at being an MP that he's about to burst out of his jacket. Moments later Jacob asked the Leader of the House, Mark Spencer, whether the votes would be free or whipped – and he replied that it would be a free vote for Tory MPs.' We all knew what that meant. The whips could not hold the line. Johnson then announced (from India) that he'd always been relaxed about it all. The Cabinet Office minister Michael Ellis adopted that approach. 'The Prime Minister has always been clear that he is happy to face whatever inquiries Parliament sees fit to hold,' he said. 'He is happy for the House to decide how it wishes to proceed today.'[2] The fact that Johnson had tabled an amendment only the night before proves this was yet another lie. The debate was serious. William Wragg was scripted and crisp. Steve Baker looked tortured as he said it was time Johnson went. Andrew Jones said he supported the investigation. The building emptied as Tory MPs melted away, and at the end of the day there was no vote because the House resolved unanimously to refer Boris Johnson to the Privileges Committee for lying. It felt like the first of many votes of no-confidence in him and his apparent disregard for the truth, which feels like his sole legacy.

A FISH ROTS FROM ITS HEAD

The list of Johnson's lies is long. He said that his original Northern Ireland Protocol would not require any paperwork for goods crossing the Irish Sea. Untrue. He said he had an 'oven-ready deal' for Brexit, which it now turns out was only half-baked. He said public sector workers had had 'significant pay increases', when their pay had actually fallen far behind inflation. One of his most often repeated lies, though, is his assertion that 'there are more people in work than there were before the pandemic began', which he repeated in parliament on twelve occasions between 24 November 2021 and 20 April 2022. The statement was categorically untrue. The chair of the UK Statistics Authority Sir David Norgrove wrote to Johnson on 24 February 2022 saying, 'According to the latest ONS figures, it is wrong to claim that there are now more people in work than before the pandemic began: the increase in the number of people who are on payrolls is more than offset by the reduction in the number of people who are self-employed.'[3] When the chair of the Work and Pensions Committee Sir Stephen Timms MP challenged Johnson on this at the Liaison Committee* hearing on 30 March, he accepted that his statements were incorrect and said, 'I have [done so] repeatedly – and I think I took steps to correct the record earlier.' When pressed on whether he *had* corrected the record, he repeated, 'I think I did, yes. I think I did.'[4] Despite these assertions, however, he had neither issued a written ministerial statement nor written to Hansard to correct the record. In fact, he subsequently repeated the inaccurate statement (after having admitted that it was inaccurate), telling the House on 20 April 2022 that there are 'more people in work than there were before the pandemic'. This was proof absolute of yet

---

*The Liaison Committee brings together the chairs of all the Commons select committees and holds regular sessions to quiz the prime minister.

another instance of his knowing, reckless and intentional misleading of parliament. He did not even correct the record about his statement to the Liaison Committee that he had corrected the record. And, lest you think this is being far too pernickety, many economists argue that one of the things that is holding the UK back is the fact that we have fewer people in the labour market now than before the pandemic. Deliberately ignoring economic facts to falsify your own record is one of the reasons we are in an economic mess. Just in case you thought Johnson was chastened by his precipitous fall from grace, it is worth remembering that even in his final speech in Downing Street he trotted out a string of falsehoods, including the claim that he had won 'the biggest majority since 1987. The biggest share of the vote since 1979.'[5] In fact, Tony Blair won larger majorities with a greater share of the vote in 1997 and 2001.

Things haven't changed much under Sunak. Take what he told the Commons on 30 November 2022, 'Straightforwardly, I was proud to support Brexit ... Let us remember one thing: we had the fastest vaccine roll-out in the world because of our freedoms after leaving the European Union.'[6] It is true that he supported Brexit, but the second half of the statement repeats a falsehood told by Johnson and Jacob Rees-Mogg. The latter told the Commons on 6 January 2022, 'I would particularly note that it is thanks to the fact that we are not in the European Union that we were able to move so quickly [with the vaccine roll-out].'[7] This is factually untrue – and a deliberately fabricated myth – for multiple reasons. For a start, the UK was still subject to EU law when the vaccines were licensed in the UK, as we were in the transition period before leaving. Secondly, the EU has expressly allowed for the UK (and other national) vaccine authorities to license vaccines independently of the European Medicines Authority ever since 2012. Thirdly, both ministers should know this because the government had stated as much in November 2020, when it issued a press release stating, 'If a suitable COVID-19 vaccine candidate ... becomes available before the end of the transition period, EU legislation which we have implemented via Regulation 174 of the Human Medicines Regulations allows the MHRA (Medicine and Healthcare products Regulatory Agency) to temporarily authorise the supply of a medicine or vaccine, based on public health need.'[8] This was repeated by the head of the MHRA, June Raine, who said, 'we have been able to authorise the supply of this vaccine using provisions under European Law which exist until 1st of January.'[9] What is more, although the first Covid vaccine was injected into an arm in England, Johnson didn't run the fastest vaccination programme even within the UK – Wales was faster. Furthermore, although the UK started well, according to the Our World in Data project at Oxford University, at the end of 2022 the UK had fully vaccinated just 76 per cent of the population.[10] By contrast, Brunei, Macau, the UAE and Qatar had managed 99 per cent; Samoa, Chile, Malta, Nicaragua and Singapore were at 90 per cent or more; Peru, Spain, Australia, New Zealand, Mauritius, Argentina, South Korea and Ecuador were at 80 per cent or more. Far from being 'world-beating', the UK languished behind forty-three other countries. It wasn't a competition – apart from with the virus – but we weren't the fastest in the world. Sunak has also been told off by the UK Statistics Authority for falsely telling the Commons that the backlog of individual asylum applications is half what it was when Labour left office. The truth is that they stood at 18,954 in June 2010 and 166,261 in 2022 when Sunak misled the House. He has still not corrected the record, despite being repeatedly asked to do so.

You might think this is an insignificant matter. I disagree. Parliament doesn't work if you can't rely on ministers to tell the truth, and the Commons has been crystal clear about the importance of ministerial honesty and correcting the record. Back in 1997, in the dying moments of John Major's government, against the background of his failed 'back to basics' campaign and countervailing sleaze, the House resolved unanimously without debate that 'It is of paramount importance that Ministers give accurate and truthful information to Parliament, correcting any inadvertent error at the earliest opportunity.'[11] Every edition of the Ministerial Code since has repeated that phrase and added, 'Ministers who knowingly mislead Parliament will be expected to offer their resignation to the Prime Minister.' The implication is clear: failing or refusing to correct the record is a resigning matter. As Professor Meg Russell has pointed out, it is especially important that ministers correct the record as they, unlike other MPs, are responsible for policy delivery, they are prominent and visible and they are substantially better resourced than other members.[12]

What is more, whereas correcting the record used to be an informal matter, it was formalised in 2007, since when ministers who spot an error write to Hansard, which then publishes their correction in a separate 'ministerial corrections' column detailing the original statement and the correction. Alternatively, if ministers want to correct the record in a more substantial way, they can issue a written ministerial statement. The Cabinet Office *Guide to Parliamentary Work* goes into considerable detail about this, insisting that corrections 'should be made in a way that is transparent and open, not only for the Member but also for others, including the general public'.[13] As Will Moy, CEO of the campaigning organisation Full Fact, told the Commons Procedure Committee, this process 'is used day in, day out, regularly without a great deal of heat or fuss. It enables important errors to be corrected.'[14] He is right. Ministers use the process hundreds of times a year. From 2007 to 2022 there were 2,714 ministerial corrections, with 268 in 2022 alone.[15] In the main these are relatively minor corrections. In 2019, for instance, Andrea Leadsom corrected the figure she had previously given for the UK's international climate finance contribution from £11.2 billion to £11.6 billion, and in November 2022 Rishi Sunak corrected his statement that '700,000 fewer children are growing up in workless households' to 600,000.[16] Nobody minds these slip-ups – and everyone respects a minister for putting them right. But the main point is, there is no excuse for a minister, let alone a prime minister, failing to correct the record.

Remarkably, Boris Johnson never once used the process as a minister, although he issued a written ministerial statement on 23 February 2022 admitting that, contrary to his assertion at Prime Minister's Questions, the government had *not* yet sanctioned Roman Abramovich.[17] Presumably he thought that an incorrect declaration that the litigious Russian oligarch and popular owner of Chelsea Football Club was *persona non grata* was worth correcting. But Johnson, Rees-Mogg and Sunak have failed and refused to correct the record about vaccination because it is an important, although fallacious, part of their self-belief. Thus the lie seeps into the body politic and others start to repeat it. Take another Johnsonism, his claim to be building 'forty new hospitals'. The junior minister

Lucy Frazer repeated this on *Question Time* on 27 October 2022, when she said, even more categorically than usual, that 'we *have* forty new hospitals'. This is at the very least misleading, as it relies on the fact that the government changed the definition of a 'new hospital' to include a 'major new clinical building on an existing site or a new wing of an existing hospital' and a 'major refurbishment and alteration of all but the building frame or main structure'.[18] In fact, fewer than half the 'new hospitals' on the Department for Health and Social Care's list constitute what any normal person would think of as a 'new hospital'. Being generous, we might suspect that Frazer was unaware of this, as she just soaked up the prime minister's assertions and parroted the Downing Street brief. But this is to stretch language so far beyond its intended meaning that one suspects Lewis Carroll was satirising a previous generation of Johnsons when Humpty Dumpty responds to Alice's objection to his mangling of the normal meaning of the word 'grand' by saying, 'When I use a word ... it means just what I choose it to mean, neither more nor less.'

CALLING OUT THE LIES

Lying – and accusing people of lying – is more complex than it might seem, as I learnt from my mother, who taught me many things. Treat everyone as you would be treated. Never judge someone by the colour of their skin, their creed, their accent or their appearance. If in doubt, be generous. One of her favourite maxims was 'If it's free, take two.' On this subject, however, she gave seemingly contradictory advice. Yes, I should always tell the truth, but no, it's not nice to call someone else a liar. It left me asking myself, wouldn't that mean the liar would get away with it?

Parliament embodies this quandary. You are never meant to impugn another 'honourable Member', so the Speaker demands MPs apologise and retract if they call an individual colleague a 'liar' or a 'hypocrite'. It is fine and dandy to call the whole of the government a bunch of liars and hypocrites, but not an individual. Likewise, you can accuse the government of presenting a false prospectus, of misleading the nation or being disingenuous. And you can make all these allegations about a named individual on television and radio or in the press to your heart's content (although you would not have the legal protection of parliamentary privilege). What you must not do on any account is say in the Commons that an individual MP is a liar, has lied, has been disingenuous or has deliberately misled the House. This can lead to bizarre contortions when a member emphasises that a colleague cannot *possibly* have *deliberately* misled the House and must have done so 'inadvertently', when we all know perfectly well that he really thinks the error was a deliberate deception.

This is not an absolute ban. The handbook to parliamentary procedure, Erskine May, clarifies that 'if a Member wishes to pursue accusations of a kind not permitted because of these principles, the proper course is to table a distinct motion about the conduct of the other Member'.[19] In other words, you can make such allegations if the debate is expressly about the conduct of another member. This was hotly debated in 2012, when Harriet Harman moved an Opposition Day motion to refer Jeremy Hunt, the then culture secretary, to the independent adviser on ministers' interests to investigate whether he had breached the Ministerial Code by failing to declare key internal government correspondence about Rupert Murdoch's bid for BSkyB. The motion mentioned paragraph 1.2c of the code (giving accurate and truthful information to parliament), so when I among others accused Hunt of deliberately lying to parliament, the Speaker rebuffed demands from Sir George Young and Jacob Rees-Mogg that I be forced to withdraw my comments. Hunt had a half-decent defence. As he put it, he wanted 'to draw the House's attention to the very important distinction between inadvertently misleading this House and lying. Lying implies that there is deliberate intent.'[20] Similarly, in the debate about whether to refer Boris Johnson to the Privileges Committee, the Speaker stated, 'while it is perfectly in order for honourable Members to question the veracity of the Prime Minister's responses to the House cited in the motion, it is not in order to challenge more generally the truthfulness of the Prime Minister or any other honourable or right honourable Member'.[21] Some reacted to the Speaker's ruling with a rolling of the eyes. After all, Johnson was never so pernickety about sticking to the rules.

The chair fiercely enforces the rule. When Dawn Butler and Ian Blackford accused Johnson of lying, they were immediately reprimanded and asked to retract. When they refused to do so, they were forced to leave the chamber and the parliamentary estate and had their pay docked for the day. If they had refused to leave, the Speaker would have formally 'named' them and (if the House agreed) they would have been suspended for five sitting days. It is a long-standing rule and I agree with the injunction that we should moderate our language, but it does seem crazy that if you accuse a member of lying, even if you are right, the person who is punished is not the liar but the person who calls it out. The most bizarre aspect of how this has played out is the fact that although the Culture Committee found in October 2022 that Nadine Dorries had misled it – when she said (as part of her attempt to denigrate Channel 4 before selling it off) that the network had used paid actors rather than real members of the public in a reality TV programme called *Tower Block of Commons* in which she had taken part, thereby implying that it was rigged – she has not been referred to the Privileges Committee, unlike the SNP MP John Nicolson, who furiously denounced the Speaker for not allowing time for a motion referring Dorries to Privileges.[22]*

The rule seems hopelessly out of sync with the British public, as polling by YouGov in 2012 suggested that nearly two-thirds of British voters agreed with the statement that 'all politicians lie all the time, and you can't trust a word they say'.[23] That was before the Johnson premiership, but more recent polling for Electoral Calculus in 2021 showed 86 per cent of voters thought that politicians who lie should lose office and in another YouGov poll in April 2022, 78 per cent thought Johnson had lied about Partygate.[24]

Two YouGov polls for the Constitution Unit in 2021 and 2022 found that the top attribute the public sought in MPs was 'be honest', ahead of 'get things done' or 'be inspiring'.[25] Yet we continue to reprimand those who call colleagues out for lying more severely than those who lie.

---

*There are ways round the rule. The smartest response to being told off for calling an MP a liar was from the playwright MP Richard Brinsley Sheridan, who was an MP between 1780 and 1812 and said, 'Mr Speaker, I said the honourable member was a liar it is true and I am sorry for it. The honourable member may place the punctuation where he pleases.'

BEING CATEGORICAL

Part of the problem is politicians' desire to be categorical. I've done it myself. We trade in certainty, not in doubt. We want to come across as authoritative and definitive, not as hesitant or tentative. We want our voice to be heard, so we turn up the volume and ratchet up the degree of certainty with which we speak. We discard nuance and abandon 'perhaps' and 'possibly' in favour of hard assertions. I know why it happens. Politics is a crowded field. The media have plenty of commentators to choose from and the sharper the clash between opposing voices the better the news item. Voters, too, like politics in bold, primary colours and seem to prefer strong vibrant figures to lead them.

In reality, the truth is not as simple as some would suggest. Sometimes it needs winkling out. Much of politics is a clash of opinions, a difference of views about how to interpret facts. One side might point to one set of facts to underpin their argument, and another might think a different set of facts is more relevant. That doesn't make either side of the argument a lie, and no political party has a monopoly on truth, however angry, passionate or certain its members are. As I said previously, one of the strengths of the British political system is that opinions, viewpoints and political claims get tested every week in the crucible of the House of Commons. And, as Jacob Rees-Mogg has repeatedly told me, just because I disagree with what he's said doesn't necessarily mean he's lying.

He's right. Two witnesses of the same event can honestly come to different conclusions. During a division about fracking on the day before Liz Truss fell, there was a sharp altercation at the entrance to the No lobby. Thanks to mixed messages from the government, including at the despatch box, several Conservatives were unsure how to vote and government whips were keen to persuade them to vote against the Labour motion as it had been termed a vote of confidence. There was quite a scrum, tempers were fraying, people were shouting and rumours were flying. No individual MP was actively bullying anyone, but to my mind it looked like a couple of MPs were being kettled into the division lobby and the overall effect was intimidatory and bullying, so I complained in the chamber. Several of my colleagues agreed and said so. But Conservative colleagues angrily disagreed and told the serjeant at arms as much when the Speaker ordered an investigation. The serjeant concluded that there was 'no evidence that anyone was bullied into voting in a particular way'.[26] I was wrong to use the term 'manhandling', but I still think the behaviour in the lobby was out of order. I also know thoroughly decent Tory whips who are deeply offended and upset by this. To them, I apologise. Sometimes we have to agree to disagree.

That being said, it is patently obvious that an overly casual or complacent attitude to verifiable, objective truth is corrosive. It inserts a bias against the truth into politics, a bit like a shopping trolley that always veers to the left. Spouting half-truths and distortions to stir up our tribe, please our core supporters and give red meat to our most ardent comrades may deliver short-term electoral advantage, but it poisons the well from which we all drink. The danger is we end up in a world where truth becomes relative and lies become normal. Never mind *the* truth, I have *my* truth and you have *yours*. Or, as has become more common in an era of social media, in which how we identify or align ourselves is more important than evidential truth, *we* have *our* truth.

Disinformation, 'alternative facts' that are not really facts at all, statistics that have been so carefully selected and manipulated that they give a false impression, images that have been cropped, altered or touched up, are utterly pernicious. And sometimes we have to assert – very categorically – that not everything that is accepted as true, even by large numbers of people, is true. The Holocaust did happen. Children were gunned down at Sandy Hook. Humans have caused climate change. Anthony Fauci and Bill Gates did not create Covid to enrich themselves. Vaccines save lives. Joe Biden won. Trump lost. Brexit has harmed our economy.

SAYING SORRY AND CORRECTING THE RECORD

Professor Benjamin Jowett, the eminent Victorian classicist who was master of Balliol College, Oxford, apparently used to advise his students, 'Never regret, never explain, never apologize. Get it over with and let them howl.'[27] Others have adopted varying versions of this motto, not least John Wayne, who drawled, 'Never apologise, mister, it's a sign of weakness', in the 1949 Western *She Wore a Yellow Ribbon*. Some have attributed the phrase to Winston Churchill and Gertrude Stein, possibly not realising that if they said it, they were quoting Jowett.[*] Whoever is to blame, it is a dire motto. Apologising when you get things wrong is a fundamental aspect of human decency. As the parliamentary commissioner for standards Daniel Greenberg has said, 'in an atmosphere where we

---

[*]A similar phrase is attributed to Napoleon: 'in politics, never retreat, never retract, never admit a mistake'. However, he is not an ideal political role model, as he also said, 'you don't reason with intellectuals, you shoot them' and 'if you wish to be a success in the world, promise everything, deliver nothing'.

treat each other with respect, you can change your mind, you can apologise without it being seen as evidence of moral turpitude'.[28] MPs hate apologising – not least because the press often derides you more for apologising than for the original misdemeanour and advisers will tell you that an apology just keeps the story running. But we need to get over ourselves and behave like adults. The Standards Committee often includes an apology to the House in a personal statement as part of a sanction – and the Speaker and I have to agree the wording of these apologies before they are made. Some colleagues are truly magnificent. They are mortified, contrite and fulsome. Others, however, quibble over every phrase and try to get away with a non-apology or make light of it. Sometimes it feels as if the member doesn't mean a word of what they're saying – as became apparent on 14 June 2021 when Daniel Kawczynski 'apologised' to the House for bullying staff, as he was required to do by the decision of the IEP. His words seemed sincere. He said that he had reflected on his behaviour, he accepted that it constituted bullying and that 'as such, [it] was entirely inexcusable'.[29] Unfortunately, he also spoke to a journalist saying in effect that he had only made the apology under duress. The Standards Committee had little choice but to impose a further sanction on him – another apology and a day's suspension. Likewise, when the Committee required another MP to apologise to the House I had to veto so many of his drafts on the grounds that they were completely unapologetic that I eventually had to threaten him with taking the matter back to the House if he did not make his apology in the precise terms required.

As one who has had to apologise many times, the point is that an apology should be an apology. It makes you a bigger person if you do it properly. The House – and the public – respects a sincere apology and despises the version that goes 'I'm sorry that you're offended' or 'I'm sorry that the Committee has found me guilty.' The corollary is that genuine apologies should be accepted at face value.*

We could do two things to improve this. Ministers are not the only MPs who make mistakes, but the sole means of correcting the record for a backbench MP is a confected one via a point of order. This, however, does not link back to the original in Hansard. Thus Sir Desmond Swayne told the House in December 2021 that more people were dying in the carnage on the roads than of Covid.[30] He admirably corrected this in a point of order the following February, but the original comments remain uncorrected in Hansard. So we should extend to all MPs, who think they have misspoken or said something that is inaccurate, the ministerial correction process, whereby ministers write to Hansard, which publishes a list of daily corrections and appends the corrected words to the original incorrect comment online. And more importantly, if a minister or a member is put on formal notification by the UK Statistics Authority that they have used statistics in an inaccurate or misleading way, the House should require the member to correct the record. If the member refuses to do so within a set period, they should automatically be considered to have breached the Code of Conduct. The question of whether someone has lied to parliament has always

_____

*Here is the text of one of my apologies, from December 2020: 'Mr Speaker, I am utterly mortified by the events of last week when my heckling interrupted proceedings during Prime Minister's questions and when I challenged the authority of the Chair. I entered into an altercation with the Chair and I did not treat the Chair with due respect. That is unacceptable. I apologise unreservedly to the House and to you personally, Mr Speaker. I really wish none of this had ever occurred and I fully accept that my conduct was unacceptable.'

been considered a matter of parliamentary privilege, adjudicated on by the Committee of Privileges, which can only consider a matter that has been referred to it by the whole House. This is inevitably a long-drawn-out process and depends on the government voting for an investigation of one of its own members – which is why it is so rarely used. In practice, that means ministers and others regularly get away with evident lies. According to Full Fact, 'As many as 50 MPs, including two Prime Ministers, Cabinet and Shadow Cabinet Ministers, failed to correct false, unevidenced or misleading claims' in 2022.[31] That's why we urgently need a simpler, speedier means of sanctioning those who mislead the House.

The Commons has already lost the battle over MPs 'marking their own homework' and the lay members of the Standards Committee are perfectly able to tell the difference between a legitimate difference of opinion and a categorical, reckless or deliberate lie, just as they adjudicate on whether an MP has brought the House into disrepute (as in the Margaret Ferrier case). That is why I would recombine the two Committees of Standards and Privileges, with seven lay members and seven MPs.

THE NECESSARY LIE

This takes me to the most difficult aspect of truth in politics. The financial journalist and founder of MoneySavingExpert. com Martin Lewis, who is said to be the most trusted man in the country, was asked at the Culture Committee's Sub-Committee on Online Harms and Disinformation on 29 November 2020 about the absence of trust in politicians. He told MPs, 'the problem with politicians isn't necessarily the individuals, it is the system. First of all, the biggest things that lack trust – collective Cabinet responsibility and the whip – are instinctively against every form of trust. You will vote for something that you don't believe in; we know you do not believe in it, we can see it.' He was very critical of the doctrine of collective Cabinet responsibility, because ministers argue for a particular policy on TV, 'and then when they are freed from the shackles – perhaps because they have a change of minister or prime minister – they will change their viewpoint'. Lewis didn't say this out of anger. He admitted that he was 'not the most robust and thick-skinned person' and that he did not know 'how any of you cope with your jobs in an adversarial situation'. But his view was clear. Collective responsibility and whipping means that party politics is rotten because it makes MPs live a lie.[32]

I understand his point. Evident inconsistency undermines confidence. When we merely parrot the whips' line, we lose our constituents' respect. In 2022 Conservative MPs were required by their government to support an increase in National Insurance Contributions introduced by Rishi Sunak, then repeal it under Liz Truss and then cheer Rishi Sunak to the rafters, all within four months. If back-pedalling were an Olympic sport they would win the team event without breaking into a sweat. It's not the first time a set of MPs has had to exercise a rapid volte-face. Queen Mary got the Commons to go down on its bended knee to ask forgiveness from Cardinal Pole for supporting the Protestant faith under her brother Edward VI, and her sister Elizabeth then got the same set of MPs to repeal Mary's repeal of Protestantism. You could also argue that Labour MPs elected on a promise not to introduce tuition fees had to perform a similarly ugly volte-face in the 2001 parliament – as did Liberal Democrats when they entered the coalition government in 2010 and trebled tuition fees in direct contradiction of their manifesto commitment. The political landscape is peppered with U-turns, and executing them with elan (and without losing half the passengers) is an important political skill.

Yet few parliaments have seen such a giddy roundabout as we have seen since 2019. Compare two statements in parliament about the UK's recent trade agreement with Australia, for instance. The first was made on 17 June 2021, the day the agreement was published: 'Australia is a very important partner of ours, and it is important that we get a trade agreement with it. It is, of course, a smaller economy and the opportunities are therefore not as large as they would be with a larger economy, but nevertheless, Australia is an important ally and this is a good agreement between us.'[33] The second came seventeen months later on 14 November 2022. 'The first step is to recognise that the Australia trade deal is not actually a very good deal for the UK ... It has to be said that, overall, the truth of the matter is that the UK gave away far too much for far too little in return.'[34] Both statements were by the same man, George Eustice, the MP for Camborne and Redruth. The only difference, as he himself admitted, is that on the first occasion he was speaking as the secretary of state for the environment, food and rural affairs, and on the second he was speaking from the backbenches as an ex-minister. The doctrine of collective responsibility, whereby ministers keep their disagreements private and always stick rigidly to the agreed party line in public, has never been so cruelly exposed. Many politicians will sympathise with Eustice. His only option if he wanted to say what he really thought back in June 2021 was to free himself from collective responsibility by resigning – and then he would have no influence on the policy at all. But others, especially sheep and beef farmers who have lost out thanks to the Australia deal, might wonder whether he refused to resign because of the £67,505 ministerial salary, the red box and the ministerial car. If so, collective responsibility is a pathetic excuse for not telling the unvarnished truth.

Yet one kind of lie is inevitable in politics. When Sir Stafford Cripps and Ernest Bevin travelled to New York in 1949 to agree a revaluation of the pound against the dollar, they had to keep the reason for their trip secret. Otherwise, there could have been a disorderly run on the pound. Even when the deal was done, they had to pretend that nothing was afoot. Cripps, who prided himself on his honesty and ethical approach to politics, was forced to lie when a journalist asked him on his arrival back in England whether he intended to devalue the pound. He felt guilty ever after, but he had no choice. Sometimes you have to lie in the national interest, a point made in 1604 by Sir Henry Wotton who said while on a delegation to Augsburg (in a much misunderstood aphorism) that an ambassador was 'an honest gentleman sent to lie abroad for the good of his country'.

THE WHIP(S)

There is one area where I agree with Martin Lewis. Some of my best friends, as they say, are whips. In all parties they spend most of their time facilitating proper debate. They feed back the views of backbench MPs to their leadership and they help MPs understand when votes will be. They are essential to the smooth running of orderly business.[*]

---

[*] The former Speaker and deputy chief whip Bernard Weatherill told my colleague Kevin Brennan, 'you can't have civilisation without sewers and you can't have parliament without the whips'.

They also look out for MPs who are ill or have to deal
with family issues. But there used to be a convention
that certain things were beyond the preserve of the
whips: House business, such as programme and recess
motions, standing order changes, the rules of the House
and disciplinary matters; anything that impinged directly
on a member's constituency; and matters of conscience.
This last category included votes on homosexuality,
abortion, the death penalty, Sunday trading, personal
freedom (for instance over smoking in public places)
and the treatment of religion. In recent years, though,
the writ of the whip has extended far further. It started
under Blair, when an equal age of consent for gay men
was a Labour Party manifesto commitment (hitherto it
had been eighteen for sex between men and sixteen for
everyone else). Suddenly all Labour MPs were expected
and required to follow the whip. Admittedly no action
was taken against Labour MPs who voted differently on
gay rights, but the expectation was there. The same has
happened under successive Conservative administrations
since 2010, as House business is now routinely whipped.
This happened most obviously over the creation of the
ICGS and the Owen Paterson report. In both cases the
whips told colleagues they were risking their careers
by voting any way other than with the prime minister.
This is nonsense. I have always liked the biblical story
of Ruth the Moabitess who stays with her Israelite
mother-in-law Naomi when her husband has died.
They are poor but manage to survive because the king's
harvesters did not reap all the way to the edge of the
field but left the gleanings for widows and orphans. We
should apply the same principle to whipping. Matters
that are central to the policy platform on which a party
stands in an election should be robustly whipped – as

should financial matters – so that voters know what they are getting when they vote for a particular party. But we should not reap to the edge of the field. MPs' consciences should be sacrosanct, and a space should be carved out for disagreement and conscientious objection. In particular, the way the Commons does its business, including how long it spends on a particular debate, changes to standing orders, motions for recess dates and disciplinary matters should never be whipped. (Incidentally, I rarely believe ministers when they assert from the despatch box that a matter is a 'free vote'. Penny Mordaunt did so repeatedly during the recent vote on the Code of Conduct, but the chief whip, Simon Hart, told me that he was busy whipping Tory MPs against my amendment which would have abolished the ministerial exception to registering hospitality; and two ministers told me they had been told they would be sacked if they voted with me. I may be wrong, but I can't help wondering whether Penny Mordaunt knew this at the time.)

Which takes me to the question that every MP gets asked in every primary school they ever visit: 'Do you always vote with your party or do you vote with your conscience?' My answer is always the same. I have very rarely voted against my party whip. The whole reason I am in the Labour Party is because its values align with mine – so my conscience and my party nearly always point in the same direction. And besides, I'm the MP for the Rhondda not because people think Chris Bryant is a wonderful chap, but because I am the Labour Party candidate. I am part of a team and it's only as part of a team that I can ever get anything done.

However, I abstained twice on secondary legislation when Labour was in government, because the regulations were improvements but too imperfect for my liking. I wish I had been less precious, as abstentions please nobody and MPs are elected to make, not avoid, decisions. My first major rebellion, though, came when Jeremy Corbyn demanded that all Labour MPs vote to trigger Article 50 to precipitate our leaving the EU. I have always been a passionate remainer and remain a remainer. I think the Leave campaign lied about what leaving would entail, but I accepted that the UK – and the Rhondda (by roughly 55/45) – had voted to leave. What I didn't accept was the wisdom of triggering Article 50 and starting a time-limited two-year process of negotiation with the EU when we had no idea what our national negotiating position should be. The Labour whips told me I could disappear for the day if I wasn't prepared to vote as instructed, but I thought that would have been cowardly, so when the Notification of Withdrawal Bill came to the Commons on 1 February 2017, I said that I would be voting in the No lobby. 'Many of my constituents will disagree with me,' I said, 'and maybe they will take it out on me, just as it was taken out on Burke in Bristol.* In the end, there is no point in any of us being a Member of this House if we do not have things that we believe in and that we are prepared to fight for and, if necessary, lay down our job for.'³⁵ I know, it sounds pompous, but I could only vote for what I believed was in the interests

---

*Edmund Burke made a brave speech to his electors in Bristol in 1774, declaring that 'it ought to be the happiness and glory of a representative to live in the strictest union, the closest correspondence, and the most unreserved communication with his constituents. Their wishes ought to have great weight with him; their opinion, high respect; their business, unremitted attention. It is his duty to sacrifice his repose, his pleasures, his satisfactions, to theirs; and above all, ever, and in all cases, to prefer their interest to his own. But his unbiased opinion, his mature judgment, his enlightened conscience, he ought not to sacrifice to you, to any man, or to any set of men living.' He rarely visited Bristol and lost the seat in 1780.

of my constituents, come what may. I received my stern rebuke from the chief whip, Nick Brown, a few days later, and it now sits in pride of place in the toilet in our home in Porth. Much to everyone's surprise, Theresa May called a general election on 18 April and I had to face an angry electorate. When we lost a majority of the council seats in the Rhondda in May, I thought my vote had done for me, but by some miracle I was re-elected on 8 June with a significantly increased majority and a nine-point swing to Labour. There were obviously other factors at play, but my breaking the whip (and voting against my constituency) did not seem to have done the lasting damage I feared.

That said, I cannot see any viable alternative to party discipline and Cabinet collective responsibility. A government isn't a government if it cannot hold itself together. As we saw in 2020–2, when party discipline collapses and MPs trawl the studios regardless of their party leader, government grinds to a halt. Ministers have to act and speak as a team. All governments come up against events and problems that stretch that unity, but Cabinet must be more than the sum of its parts. If it collapses into individuals rutting like stags, it would be better off handing back the keys to Downing Street. Politicians have egos (I include myself in this), but the endless parading of individuals' consciences and opinions – and the consequent buffeting of the ship of state hither and thither on the high seas of public opinion – is far worse than the compromises inherent in collective responsibility. And besides, it is always open to a minister to resign. Honourable resignations – like Lord Carrington over the Falklands or Robin Cook over Iraq – are rare these days, notwithstanding the flurry of last-minute (or last-straw) resignations that forced Boris Johnson out of office. I accept that nobody likes a minister endlessly threatening to resign and self-righteously parading their conscience all over the place and everyone prefers a team player. But perhaps that's where the issue lies. Surrendering power, influence, income and authority is unattractive, especially if parliament seems irrelevant except as a means to becoming a minister. Which is yet another reason why parliament needs to rediscover its own identity and take the power of initiative back from the executive. If being a minister is the be all and end all of politics, honourable resignations over matters of conscience will be scarce. If parliament can become again a crucible of national debate, a body that seeks to devise solutions to the nation's problems, a legislature that holds its timetable in its own hands, then ministers might not fear becoming ex-ministers so much.

One final point on truthfulness, the whips and party discipline. Much as I respect the solitary Green MP Caroline Lucas, the singleton is rarely successful in British politics because you can't win a vote in the Commons, you can't change the law and you can't form a government as a band of one. True, politics is nothing without personal conviction, but the art of politics is creating alliances, building momentum and sustaining a team. Individual egos have to be suppressed to achieve a common purpose. That is why we have political parties. In the main they keep politicians honest, unlike in the USA where party discipline is weak and Congress members' votes are up for grabs to the highest bidder. The idea of a House entirely consisting of free-floating independent MPs, elected without a party and with no allegiance, is fanciful and dangerous. Much more important is the *independently minded* MP, who knows when to think for herself or push her cause, and when to join the crowd.*

Some want more radical solutions to the problem of parliamentary mendacity. A total of 133,007 people signed up to a petition calling for a new criminal offence of lying to parliament as an MP. The Plaid MP, Liz Saville Roberts, has introduced the Elected Representatives (Prohibition of Deception) Bill which goes further. It would fine and bar from office a politician who made any kind of public pronouncement which they knew to be misleading, false or deceptive. It sounds attractive. Perjury (lying to a court of law) is a serious offence, so why not lying to parliament? My fear is that such a law would drag the police and CPS into daily allegations and counter-allegations about who said what and force them to make essentially political decisions about what constituted a manifest, significant, wilful or reckless lie.

That brings me back to Boris Johnson and the Privileges Committee. He said he was relaxed about it when it was set up, but spent most of his time attacking it. When giving oral evidence, he looked pink and got cross. He relied on the flimsiest of excuses. A single member of staff had assured him it was all right. He didn't deny joking that Downing Street was the 'least unsocially distanced' space in Britain.[36] He was such a good boss that he wanted to thank staff at leaving dos. People were working very hard. They had tried their best. None of this seems to wash with the public. The polls suggest that the vast majority think

---

*Richard Brinsley Sheridan was equally unimpressed when his son Tom said that if he got into parliament he would not pledge himself to any party, but would write on his forehead, 'To Be Let'. Sheridan replied 'And under it, Tom, write, "Unfurnished".'

that he lied to parliament about partying in Downing Street and that he lied to the Committee about whether he had lied to parliament. People thought the whole point of the national pandemic response was that we were all in this together, so they feel visceral anger that this was the biggest lie of all. As one lad told me in the sports centre at Ystrad, 'If Boris gets away with all those lies, there's no point in voting any more.'

But he didn't get away with it. The Committee concluded that he intentionally misled the House in fourteen different ways. It recommended that he be suspended for 90 days for 'deliberately misleading the House, deliberately misleading the Committee, breaching confidence, impugning the Committee and thereby undermining the democratic process of the House and being complicit in the campaign of abuse and attempted intimidation of the Committee.'[37] That is a shocking charge sheet. Rather than face the music in the Commons or in his constituency, Johnson resigned as an MP in a burst of self-pity and narcissism moments after receiving the draft report, but not before the publication of his discredited resignation honours list. Rather than answer the charges, he cynically attacked the integrity of the committee. He still has his defenders, most of whom have received honours from him. Newly knighted Jacob Rees-Mogg, the man who led the Commons into a deep moral crevasse over Owen Paterson, still proclaims his virtue. But the fact remains that Johnson left in disgrace, found guilty of lying by his peers. The process was laborious, but thanks to the tenacity of the committee members, parliament asserted that it does have standards. On 19 June 2023, the Commons voted 354:7 to agree the report. The only disturbing fact? 227 Tory MPs did not vote, including Sunak. Have they learnt nothing?

5

Conduct Unbecoming

Even the most senior public figures are entitled to a private life and I despise that illogical combination of prurience and self-righteousness that seems to drive the tabloid obsession with MPs' (plus actors' and footballers') sex lives. That's why I never want to return to the judgemental and often hypocritical moral code of our forebears. But some aspects of the way MPs conduct themselves, including in private, are a proper matter of public concern. Bullying, harassment and sexual misconduct are inappropriate in any workplace. They are totally unacceptable in Parliament.

This is, however, a relatively new understanding, as views on what constitutes acceptable behaviour have changed rapidly. Less than a hundred years ago Sir Henry Curtis-Bennett, one of the most celebrated defence barristers in the land, decided to step down from parliament when his wife's solicitor told him that there was sufficient evidence for her to sue for divorce, because divorce was considered socially and politically improper. Many others saw their political careers founder thanks to affairs of the heart. Sir Charles Dilke was thought of as a possible future leader of the Liberals until he was caught up in a divorce case in 1885, and the charismatic leader of the Irish Nationalist Party, Charles Stewart Parnell, rode high until he was cited as co-respondent in the divorce of his long-term lover Kitty O'Shea. One of the many enigmas of political life has always been how some such affairs are splashed over the tabloids and others – even though they are the talk of the Commons tearoom and the Strangers' Bar – never appear in a newspaper. Many prime ministers flourished despite complex (not to say curious, or at least not entirely monogamous) private lives, including Palmerston, Melbourne, Rosebery, Gladstone and Lloyd George. The situation for homosexuals was even more restrictive, as sodomy, gross indecency and importuning for immoral purposes (under the Vagrancy Acts) were all criminal offences, and in the Royal Navy and the British Army 'conduct unbecoming an officer and a gentleman' would see an officer court-martialled and cashiered. Some gay MPs managed to live secret double lives within a tight coterie of like-minded friends, but when David Maxwell Fyfe was home secretary and lord chancellor between 1951 and 1962, he was keen to secure arrests, prosecution and convictions to 'rid England of this male vice … this plague'. He also told the Commons that 'homosexuals in general are exhibitionists and proselytisers and are a danger to others, especially the young.'[1] Ironically enough, those arrested included two Conservative MPs, William Field, the MP for Paddington North, and Ian Harvey, the MP for Harrow West, who were respectively convicted of importuning for immoral purposes and gross indecency with a Coldstream guardsman (neither of which offences still exists today). Both were forced to resign.

Hypocrisy abounded. The wealthy often got away with greater 'sins' against the moral code of the day (or the newspaper editors' public version of it) because they had higher walls behind which to enjoy their privacy. Nancy Astor, for instance, kept her son's arrest, court-martial, discharge and imprisonment for homosexuality out of the press partly thanks to her husband owning several newspapers. None of this is true today, thank goodness. The King is a remarried divorcee, as are many MPs. Homosexuality is legal and we have at least sixty-one LGBT MPs. Some even boast of their Grindr profile. Most people respect MPs' right to a private life and the press are rightly cautious of publishing a story outing a Cabinet minister as gay or revealing an adulterous affair. Consensual sex outside a heterosexual marriage is no longer a bar to being an MP, and I am delighted that today's parliament would never contemplate a three-hour debate on 'moral values' such as that led by Sir Hal Miller in 1989, when MPs pontificated about the Church abandoning 'the eternal for the obviously temporal' (and condemned 'homosexual marriage').[2]

Times, as the song goes, have changed in other ways, too. When I was first elected in 2001 it was not uncommon for an older male MP to slap a younger female (or male) MP on the backside in the tearoom or the division lobby, but complaints about sexually inappropriate behaviour – if anyone ever dared to make one – were always dealt with in secret by the whips. Everything was swept under the very elegant Pugin carpet. Of course, some predatory, handsy men took advantage of this culture of impunity. I remember very clearly in my first few weeks seeing the look on a young female colleague's face when a drunken Cabinet minister lunged at her, hugged her tight and felt her bottom in the division lobby against her will. She looked sickened – and frightened. All we did was avoid him in the future. Things were little better for gay men. Over the years five male MPs have felt my bottom uninvited. One of them, who was not out, did so repeatedly. Another, who is still in the House and still does not accept that he is gay, pushed me against a wall and felt my crotch. Another rubbed himself behind me in the queue to vote and was later snogging two men in the Strangers' Bar. I know other gay MPs and staff who have faced the same. Again, we did nothing. We never complained.

Things are somewhat better today. In July 2018 the two Houses signed up to the Parliamentary Behaviour Code and created the Independent Complaints and Grievance Scheme (ICGS). This deals in confidence with complaints about bullying, harassment and sexual misconduct within the parliamentary community. The ICGS investigates complaints and if the parliamentary commissioner for standards upholds a complaint against an MP, he sends it to the Independent Expert Panel (IEP), which was set up in June 2020 and started work that November under the chairmanship of a former High Court judge, Sir Stephen Irwin. The IEP determines the appropriate sanction, which can include temporary suspension or permanent exclusion, and hears appeals against the commissioner's decision and the sanction. This was long overdue – and it is not perfect – but ours is the first legislature in the world to have such a confidential system and we should be proud that people like Andrea Leadsom, Harriet Harman, Stella Creasy and Jess Phillips campaigned for it and the whole House voted for it. Sadly, though, we still haven't got this right, as evidenced by the fact that many staffers find parliament an unsafe place to work. When Unite in 2022 surveyed its members who work in parliament, 33 per cent said they had heard about or witnessed sexual misconduct towards another member of staff from an MP, and 20 per cent had experienced bullying or harassment from their boss.[3] I cannot think of any other commercial or public sector organisation that would return similar statistics.

Again, in the interests of full disclosure, it would be wrong of me to proceed without full transparency about my own misdemeanours. I was single back in 2003 and used the online dating app Gaydar to meet people. I'm not quite sure how it all came to light, but the *News of the World* hacked my phone at the time and in November the *Mail on Sunday* knocked on my door with a photo I had taken of myself in the bathroom mirror, dressed in my 2(X)IST underpants. It had never been available for all and sundry to see online, but I had sent it to someone who had then given it to the paper. The *Mail on Sunday* published a YouGov poll about me the next week. Only 17 per cent thought I should resign, 29 per cent thought I had done nothing wrong and 69 per cent thought I had a right to a private life. I have never felt so terrible and I hardly slept for two months, which is why I often drop a quick note to MPs who get into scrapes saying 'chin up and *nil carborundum*' (don't let the buggers grind you down). But I now like to joke that I invented the selfie, that I don't look anywhere near as buff today as I did then and that I increased my majority at the next election, so it pays to advertise. I also note that several MPs and journalists use similar dating apps today without anyone fretting. Hurrah!

What follows therefore does not come with any sanctimony. I do not care who has sex with whom, nor what kind of sex they engage in, so long as it is on the basis of fully informed consent and does not abuse a position of authority or trust. The old court-martial offence of 'conduct unbecoming an officer and a gentleman' relied on a social code that looked askance at dishonesty, indecency, lawlessness, indecorum, injustice and cruelty, less because they were inherently wrong and more because they were 'in bad taste' and might bring the unit into disrepute. Homosexuality and marital infidelity offended that code, but improper advances to a staff member and manifest bullying were ignored. What the #MeToo movement – and the subsequent scandals in parliament – showed was that we needed to turn those assumptions on their head.

WHY PARLIAMENT STILL HAS A PROBLEM

Parliament's unusual (although not unique) working environment means that it has several problems when it comes to the nexus of bullying, harassment and sexual misconduct.

For a start, the emotional fulcrum of parliament turns on patronage and power. Everyone is seeking promotion, including MPs, researchers, secretaries, special advisers and office managers. The PPS wants to be a junior minister, the researcher wants to be a special adviser. Titles abound (and I say this as a newbie knight bachelor). Sir, dame, honourable, right honourable, chairman, lord president, baroness, viscount. I would love to be able to say that the key to prospering in politics is diligence and ability. But just as often it depends on being a good social performer, currying favour with your boss and other MPs and burnishing your reputation for being helpful and cooperative. Sharp elbows matter as much as sharp intellect, if not more. An eye for the main chance can help – as long as you manage to massage others' egos as gently as your own. This may be true in all office politics, but parliamentary politics is fundamentally social and being 'difficult' may see you marked down or ostracised, which probably deters people from complaining about inappropriate behaviour.

There is some good news. This used to be worse. Everything used to reinforce the hierarchy. Even the cafeteria and the post office gave preference to MPs and allowed them to queue-barge. Most of that has gone, but some colleagues still behave as if parliament belongs to them and owes them deference at every turn. Even thoroughly decent, well-intentioned MPs can become overly demanding or forget that they are in a position of power.* Their sharp witticisms might be fine between two equal colleagues but can be profoundly wounding when addressed to an employee. Likewise, it may be flattering when a young researcher seems fascinated by everything an MP has to say, but the MP (like in any other profession) has to be aware of their position of authority and should avoid abusing it. A member of staff may be too frightened to say 'no', too anxious about their career to make a complaint. So the onus always has to be on MPs, in the words of the Behaviour Code: 'recognise your power, influence or authority and don't abuse them'.

There's another factor that hinders parliament getting this right. MPs' previous experience varies enormously. Some have extensive experience of employing people and have led large multidisciplinary teams. Others have never employed a single person beforehand – or have only employed someone in a family firm or an environment where working practices are completely different from the public sector. It is not unknown, for instance, for

---

*I have only once heard an MP say 'Do you know who I am?', but the friendly Conservative MP Edward Timpson, who is retiring at the next election, tells me that he used the phrase once. He was on a very drunken pub-crawl stag party and found himself trying to get into a Park Lane hotel bar at the end of the night, only to be rebuffed by the doorman on the grounds that he was drunk and was not resident at the hotel. 'Do you know who I am?' he said, adding that his father had a suite at the Dorchester. 'That's all very well, sir, but this is the Hilton,' came the reply.

someone who successfully built their own firm to require a staff member to buy their partner's Christmas presents, pick the children up from school or prepare their food. That might be fine in a private company, but is it right in parliament? Likewise, as long as you abide by the law, it's up to you how you select your staff when it's your own company. But it's a bit different when the taxpayer is footing the bill. I know some people believe that talking about 'unconscious bias' is political correctness gone mad, but in my experience most MPs would be more than happy to have proper HR training, advice and support when employing staff. Parliament, after all, should be an exemplar of best practice, not the final resting place of outdated work practices. Yet some MPs appoint staff without open advertisement, they interview alone and they ask questions like 'Do you intend to get pregnant?' Weeding out our private prejudices – or at least helping us to understand them – is an important part of making sure we employ staff on the basis of merit and don't always employ someone who looks like us. That is why every MP should only be allowed to employ staff with taxpayers' money through IPSA if they have undertaken employment training, they have held an openly advertised competition and they are accompanied at interview by a colleague or a human resources specialist. (Enforced training is not ideal. When I did the Commons Valuing Everyone course, I was struck that several peers seemed to have completely antediluvian views that would have frightened Genghis Khan.)

In addition, MPs are reluctant to report or even refer to inappropriate behaviour by a colleague. In part that is because of our national British reluctance to interfere in anyone else's business. Our home is our castle. Our

office is our business and nobody else's. We prefer to be
discreet. One historic incident perhaps explains this best.
The Liberal government was having a massive row with
the House of Lords over Lloyd George's revolutionary
budget in 1911. There had been three general elections
in as many years. The prime minister, H. H. Asquith,
needed to win a vote in the Commons on a key
amendment to the Parliament Bill. But he was blind
drunk and could barely get his words out. His opposite
number Arthur Balfour commented on his 'very strange
performance'[4] and begged ministers to take him home.*
Winston Churchill (who was then a Liberal) said he
'squirmed with embarrassment' and thought that 'only
the persistent freemasonry of the House of Commons
prevents a scandal'.[5] Freemasons object to this term
(my apologies), but such 'freemasonry' is a common
aspect of the parliamentary rumour mill. People prefer
to gossip rather than address inappropriate behaviour
head-on. Often, for fear of giving their political party
a problem, MPs prefer to deal with things privately –
or not at all. Take this instance. *Politico* published the
following story in December 2022: 'One former
Conservative MP, now a member of the House of
Lords, asked hosts for directions to the nearest brothel
when he travelled to Southeast Asia on a visit with an
all-party parliamentary group (APPG), according to
another parliamentarian who was present. Another
Tory MP and former minister used to stay on after the
MPs' delegation had returned home in order to pursue
his "interest in [local] women," two former colleagues
said.'[6] In another story, it was said that MPs had been

---

*'Squiffy' already meant mildly intoxicated before Asquith joined the Commons,
but his reputation meant he was known affectionately as 'Old Squiffy'.

horrified to see a colleague repeatedly make unwanted advances to young interns on overseas trips. This kind of behaviour – if true – is manifestly inappropriate. It might even constitute a criminal offence. But the answer is not to tell a journalist about it. No amount of churning the rumour mill is going to change the working culture or protect vulnerable individuals.* Leadership – one of the Nolan Principles – requires us all to call out bad behaviour where we see it and when we see it. Every time we fail to do so, we collude with bad behaviour and we further tarnish parliament's reputation. That is why I commend the Tory women MPs who reported Neil Parish for watching porn in the chamber in front of them. And those who reported Chris Pincher's behaviour at the Carlton Club. Gossip – much of it third and fourth hand – might get a good headline in the media, but it damages parliament's reputation without bringing about change. In particular, in the instance where MPs witnessed a colleague repeatedly hitting on a young intern, the right thing to do was either confront the MP and/or report it to the ICGS. Failing to do one or the other is an act of quiet collusion.

This takes me to the matter of employing family members. I have never been convinced that this practice helps. I have heard all the arguments in favour. Colleagues point out that a partner or child will probably work many more hours than their contract specifies, and many marriages are a close political partnership. They believe working together maintains a happy family life in a difficult circumstance. But if a junior staff member

---

*Several newspapers reported in 2022 that fifty-four (or 'more than 50') MPs were under investigation for bullying, harassment or sexual misconduct. I said this was untrue at the time but journalists repeatedly called me a liar. I was right. I condemn any such misconduct but exaggeration does not help anyone.

is feeling uncomfortable with their MP, they may feel that they have nowhere to go if their direct manager is the MP's spouse or daughter. However, since 2017, IPSA has banned MPs from employing any new 'connected parties', so the number is dwindling and the practice will probably have ended within a decade.

Another aspect of parliament that adds to the risk of inappropriate behaviour is the fact that modern politics is a bit like living in a goldfish bowl that could turn into a slow cooker at any moment. The pressure is intense. The media round turns like the fastest gyroscope. One minute you are preparing for a serious debate on pension reform, the next you are responding to a Twitter storm (or deciding to ignore it) or a constituency crisis. MPs are balancing competing demands on a daily basis. MPs are also now far easier to contact – by phone, email, WhatsApp, text, direct messages on Twitter, Facebook, messenger and countless other apps. Familiarity has bred a degree of contempt. And normally it is not the MP but the staff member (rather like the GP surgery receptionist) who bears the brunt of the abuse. The sheer quantity of messages and phone calls can be overwhelming and some MPs undoubtedly pass their sense of frustration on to their staff. Many years ago, I regularly found my next-door MP's chief of staff sitting outside their office in floods of tears – and sometimes as you walk down one of the corridors you hear an MP bawling out abuse at their staff. Occasionally I've had the courage to talk to a colleague about it – but not often enough.

The turnover of MPs' staff is also high. This may be partly because budgets are tight and pay is not competitive. A researcher can often earn far more after a couple of years spent in an MP's office working for a lobbying firm or a charity, so they move on. But some MPs have a problem and must spend many hours interviewing staff, as they get through so many. Most MPs are caring, careful, considerate employers who only want to get the best out of their staff. However, a few of my colleagues are notoriously bad, as the recent survey by Unite and another by the GMB showed.[7] Shockingly, 17 per cent of staff who had previously worked for another MP said they had been forced to move because of bullying, and 62 per cent said they had witnessed or heard of bullying or harassment towards another colleague. A small majority – 52 per cent – felt able to raise these matters with their MP, but over a third felt they couldn't. One staff member told the GMB, 'The closer we came to an election ... the more short-tempered and more unreasonable [the employer] became in her interactions with me and her constituency staff ... All of the issues noted above were exacerbated by the fact that the MP's only senior and longstanding member of staff – her office manager – was also her husband.'[8] When Lee Anderson posted details of one of his staff member's pay and personal finances to prove a point about low incomes, many pointed out that he had the seventh highest staff turnover in parliament – beaten by Claudia Webbe, Katherine Fletcher, Louie French, Neil Hudson, Chi Onwurah and Chris Loder.[9] There may be many exceptional circumstances that lead to such a situation and I am not suggesting any of the above have behaved badly towards their staff, but an MP that gets through large numbers of staff year after year needs help (as, almost certainly, do their staff). IPSA should offer additional HR support and training to MPs with a high staff-turnover rate.

Besides, MPs owe a duty of care to their staff. Often a researcher (either in Westminster or in the constituency) will be working alone or with just one other staff member most of the day, as their MP is in the chamber or in committee. This can be very isolating. I know one MP who works almost entirely from their home in the constituency. They attend parliament only to speak or to vote. This leaves their parliamentary researcher working alone for more than 80 per cent of the time. That may be fine for a gregarious, confident, well-balanced and well-connected individual. But it could all too easily lead to mental health problems. The fact that an MP's office is a separate tight-knit unit means this is not a healthy way to work – and parliament needs to do far more to create buddying networks so that individuals are not isolated.

It may seem a technical point, but another factor that contributes to parliament's strange workplace culture is the fact that MPs are formally speaking office-holders rather than employees and each MP effectively runs a small business. MPs' offices in parliament reinforce this sense of there being 650 separate employment units. Many place the MP and staff far from view behind heavy wooden doors. Only a few have a shared space with another MP. The offices have been designed for privacy, but privacy can be abused.

Moreover, parliament can still feel like an old boys' reunion dinner, not least because only a smidgen over a third of MPs in the 2019 parliament are women (224 out of 650). A recent report by the Fawcett Society found that 69 per cent of women MPs and 49 per cent of men had witnessed sexist behaviour in parliament in the previous five years, and only 37 per cent of women and 55 per cent of men agreed that the culture in parliament is inclusive for people like them.[10] Most disturbingly, it also found that 62 per cent of women MPs felt that parliamentary culture had a negative impact on how they feel about being an MP (compared to 34 per cent for men), which may explain why many retire earlier or leave parliament after a briefer spell than their male counterparts. Of course, as the allegations about Priti Patel show, women can also be bullies. Statistics are hard to come by, but the Workplace Institute found that 80 per cent of women that are bullied in the workplace are bullied by other women. Women can also engage in sexually inappropriate behaviour, but we won't change the culture in parliament until we reach equality.

Finally, I understand why personal loyalty and discretion are highly valued commodities in an MP's office. Election and re-election feel very personal to the MP. But we can all get into bad habits. Pride in getting elected and a sense of the privilege of office can turn the best-set head. One gay MP recently told me, 'I have only ever employed gay men, how else could I rely on their discretion?' So I would welcome a requirement for MPs to have a confidential external mentor or a regular refresher course on employment best practice. Some MPs are better at coping with pressure than others and some have other external pressures weighing down on them. Yes, parliament has an excellent Health and Wellbeing Service, which has provided increasing levels of support for MPs and staff. The Individual Assistance Programme also provides a twenty-four-hour independent and confidential mental health support service for MPs, with which MPs made 1,197 appointments between 2016 and 2019 (when House of Commons staff made 7,608 appointments for the equivalent Employee Assistance Programme).[11] But MPs need support if they are to cope with the intense pressure of the job. That will mean confidentially helping an MP and staff member work through a difficult problem long before it has festered into bitterness and rancour.

More importantly, attitudes need to change. I don't suppose a single MP would ever admit it, but once you've made it to parliament or become a minister it is all too easy to develop the swagger of entitlement, to feel one is the cock of the walk and to expect deference from those who work for you. I cringed when Johnson's acolytes referred to him as 'big dog', but many MPs spend much of their time managing upwards, seeking promotion or trying to avoid being sacked. Thus entitlement cascades down the chain of command and mutual respect disappears into thin air.

IS EVERYONE JUST FAR TOO SENSITIVE?

Definitely not. The cases that have already been decided by the ICGS since it came into existence in 2018 make clear that some MPs – albeit a very small number – have no idea what is appropriate behaviour.

Take the case of Mike Hill, who was Labour MP for Hartlepool. He had known the woman concerned before he was elected and offered her a well-paid job without any recruitment process or competition. Despite the fact that he was married, he also offered her subsidised accommodation in a one-bedroom flat in London to be shared with him, and texted her to say 'I also crave your body.' She made it clear that she did not want a sexual relationship, but agreed to share the flat on a temporary basis, with him sleeping on the couch and her in the bedroom. On one occasion he attempted to get into bed with her. And he came up behind her on many occasions in his parliamentary office and touched her inappropriately.[12] Hill resigned before the IEP published its conclusions, but he would undoubtedly have faced a serious sanction had he remained.

The IEP has also found against Rob Roberts, the Conservative MP for Delyn, for making repeated and unwanted sexual advances towards a member of staff. It also agreed with the parliamentary commissioner for standards that the SNP's Patrick Grady 'had, under the influence of alcohol, made an unwanted sexual advance to the complainant that included the touching and stroking of the complainant's neck, hair, and back'.[13] In that case eight other complaints were not upheld. Most recently, they also found that the Labour MP for Chester, Christian Matheson, had issued a sexually motivated and unwanted invitation to a junior member of his staff to take a private trip to Gibraltar with him, and had placed her under pressure and intimidated her. In addition he had taken her to a work-related dinner, 'and during the evening linked arms with her; made personal comments about her appearance while looking at her suggestively; made her hold his hand as they left and insisted on accompanying her to her bus stop; and once there invited her back to his flat, kissed her twice on the forehead and attempted to kiss her on the mouth'.[14] The IEP decided to suspend Matheson for four weeks, but he too resigned before the requisite motion was put to the House.

In one sense – bear with me – this is all good news. I do not doubt for an instant that very similar conduct to this had been happening in parliament for centuries. The difference is, we are now taking it seriously as an abuse of power, of trust and of privilege. There have been occasional slips. It was clearly wrong of Theresa May to give the Conservative whip back to Andrew Griffiths and Charlie Elphicke in time for them to participate in a vote of confidence in her in December 2018. Both had been suspended over serious allegations of inappropriate sexual behaviour. The former was later revealed to have raped his wife[15] and the latter was convicted on three counts of sexual assault. Restoring the whip gave the impression that parliament did not care about these matters, as did the fact that five Conservative MPs tried to have witness statements relating to Elphicke's case kept secret.

There is one final and very important point. Some MPs neither understand nor accept that their behaviour is inappropriate. They admit they are 'demanding'. They confess that they push their staff hard and expect a very high standard of performance. If that is all it is, then fine. So too is an occasional grumpy mood or a sharp tone of voice. But all too often MPs get into terrible habits and soon their demands are exorbitant and out of all proportion, their tone is permanently derogatory or peremptory and the poor staff member is a quivering wreck. Occasional bouts of excessive praise don't help either, as the staff member is left feeling frightened of what will greet them the next time they see their boss. Will it be lavish praise or harsh criticism? Will they be up or down? If your staff feel they are walking on eggshells or permanently on tenterhooks, you're probably a bully.

TAKING PRECAUTIONS

As I said earlier, the vast majority of MPs know how to treat their staff and everyone they work with respectfully. They can also spot behaviour that is out of order. But the culture in parliament is still not as professional as it should be. Our working practices are still archaic. And many staff still don't think it is as safe a place to work as we would all want. That needs to change.

One reform that is overdue relates to MPs who are arrested, bailed or charged with serious sexual or violent crimes. Most other workplaces would take precautionary action in such circumstances, either restricting the employee's work pattern or suspending them from work pending investigation. Nothing should compromise the principle that one is innocent until proven guilty and no such action should ever imply guilt. It must be a genuinely neutral act and it must be proportionate. But, just as it makes sense for a prime minister to be able to suspend a minister pending investigation (see p. 43), it is wrong that we have no such system in parliament. This is not simple, not least because constituents should not lose out from a precautionary suspension of their MP and we don't want to incentivise partisan vexatious allegations. But the police already notify the clerk of the House whenever an MP is arrested (even for traffic offences), so we should introduce a system whereby the clerk nominates an officer of the House to assess in each case whether any actions need to be taken to protect other members of the parliamentary community (for instance by moving the member to an open-plan office, or barring the member from the Commons bars or from overseas travel). In most cases no action will be needed, but in some extreme cases it might be necessary to suspend the member from parliament pending investigation, which would require a vote of the House. I understand colleagues' reluctance – and this may be a measure we would only use when a member is publicly charged with a serious offence – but it is time we became an early adopter of best practice on this, not laggards.

We also have to do something about the physical environment of parliament. Leaving aside the dangers of fire and flood (and the fact that some MPs refuse to tackle the problems in the building because they don't want the inconvenience of moving out), the building was designed for a different era and facilitates poor behaviour. It has endless warrens and nooks and crannies. Most offices are cribbed and cabined, with staff pressed up against each other and their MP in close quarters and behind thick doors. The only staff who work in open-plan and open-to-view offices work for the House rather than for individual MPs. (The kitchens, incidentally, are extraordinarily cramped and it is a miracle more staff don't complain about the heat, the lack of ventilation and the lack of personal space. The same is true for the accommodation for security staff.) Contrary to rumour, there are not 'dozens' of bars in parliament, but there are five restaurants (Strangers, Members, Peers, Churchill, Adjournment), four cafeterias (Bellamy's in 1 Parliament Street, the Debate in Portcullis House, the Terrace cafeteria in the main palace and Portcullis in 7 Millbank) and the following bars or lounges: the Pugin Room, the Strangers' Bar, the Smoking Room (where you cannot smoke) and the Bishops' Bar in the Lords. MPs also have a tearoom (with Labour and Tory ends) and journalists have the cheerless and unwelcoming Moncrieff's Café Bar, although most of them prefer to mingle and earwig with MPs. There is also the bizarre Sports and Social Club, which was for ages run by a separate company. Not long after I was first elected it was temporarily closed following an investigation featuring a peer of the realm and a prostitute.

There is a reason for all these catering venues. Nearly 12,000 people have parliamentary passes, including builders, contractors, clerks, cleaners, MPs, peers and their staff. It is a vast army that moves on its stomach. Many staff are poorly paid and like any half-decent employer parliament tries to ensure there is nutritious food at an affordable price for them. Alcohol is also readily available – and if you really want to, as an MP, you can get free beer and wine at a reception or a dinner (or courtesy of a journalist's or lobbyist's generous expense account) pretty much any day of the working week. Several reception rooms are designed specifically to host such events, including the State Rooms in Speaker's House, the Jubilee Room, the IPU Room, the Cholmondeley Room, the Attlee Suite and a string of dining rooms off the Terrace.

Late-night sessions in the chamber are rarer than they used to be. In my early days we often finished at 1 or 2 a.m., and members gathered in the bars waiting for votes. Some got paralytic. One Tory, who is no longer an MP, tried to have a conversation with me in Strangers' Bar about our differences on Europe, but kept on falling off his stool and never made it to the vote. That same night a new female Tory MP was so drunk that when the serjeant at arms offered to give her a hand she was sick all over her. The Tory MP Tracey Crouch has said how much she hates the atmosphere this engenders. 'I became quite upset,' she told Gloria De Piero on GB News, 'quite disillusioned by the number of people going through division lobbies reeking of booze. It's just not a pleasant environment.' She added that she has seen colleagues miss votes or vote the wrong way because of alcohol.

I don't want to be too pious about this. I am a regular in the Strangers' Bar and the Smoking Room. I never drink before speaking in the chamber or doing a radio or TV interview, but I like chewing the cud with friends and colleagues over a pint or a glass (or several) of wine. Politics is, after all, a social and sociable profession. Sharing food and drink is part of cementing a friendship or an alliance. And I remember the first time I bumped into Tony Blair after I was elected in 2001. I had gone out to dinner with a colleague who had just split up from his wife. He was drinking heavily – and later quit booze altogether – and we downed three bottles between us. He probably consumed more than I did, but I was squiffy by the time I arrived at the A-G desk in the No lobby (where clerks crossed off our names before the electronic pass readers were introduced), immediately behind Blair. We chatted – or at least I tried to chat – but he seemed singularly unimpressed.

However, the excessive consumption of alcohol is far less common than it used to be. When I first entered the Commons there was a group of MPs who would take their places in the Sports and Social Club the moment it opened, at 11 a.m., and would stay there till the end of the day. Back then, if you invited an MP to lunch, he might down a cocktail or two before swigging a bottle or more of wine and would then return to the Commons, which started at 2.30 in the afternoon. No wonder several died of alcoholism. All that is gone. Most MPs would not dream of touching a drop at lunchtime. Many never drink in parliament and avoid the bars like the plague. That doesn't stop some journalists from manufacturing fibs about MPs. Henry Deedes, for instance, writing about President Zelensky's speech in Westminster Hall after PMQs in February 2023, wrote in the *Daily Mail*, 'Usually at this hour, most members are heading to the bars for post-PMQs snifters.'[16] I have never known an

MP go to the bar at midday on a Wednesday, or any other day, and the idea that more than 325 would do so is utter nonsense. Sadly, a few incidents have given the bars a bad reputation – most notably when Eric Joyce assaulted Stuart Andrew in the Strangers' Bar in 2012 – but the likely effect of closing them all would be that the drinking would move out of sight and off the estate, and that might be worse.

THE LOBBIES

The division lobbies are every bit as dangerous as the bars. Let me explain. We vote in the House of Commons in two ways, by acclamation or by division. It starts with the Speaker putting the question at the end of the debate by saying, 'All those in favour, say "Aye", and then 'All those opposed shout "No".' If nobody shouts 'No', or if there are obviously many more people shouting 'Aye', the Speaker says, 'I think the Ayes have it', and we proceed to the next business. That is a vote by acclamation. If, however, there are further shouts of 'Aye' or 'No', the Speaker calls a division, saying, 'Clear the lobbies', and division bells start ringing around the parliamentary estate to summon members for the vote. Members have eight minutes to get into a division lobby.

When the eight minutes are up, the Speaker shouts, 'Lock the doors.' The doorkeepers are dressed ornamentally in white tie and tails, but they take this instruction literally, ferociously slamming the lobby doors shut. Often a straggler is left out of puff and irritated that she has failed to vote. Inside the division lobbies we have a few minutes in which to tap our passes on a pass reader to record our vote before passing through a narrow door to be counted through by the tellers for the Ayes and the Nos. When everyone is through, the four tellers (two Aye and two No) come back into the chamber, and the winning side gives the result to the clerks before taking their place in front of the table. The House knows who has won because the winning tellers face the Speaker standing on the right (by the Opposition benches). They then announce the numbers, which are repeated by the Speaker before instructing 'Unlock.'

The division lobbies, which are little more than corridors, are crowded, with MPs jostling up against each other, often after dinner and late at night. As I said above, I have seen more inappropriate behaviour here than anywhere else on the estate. Older male MPs slapping women's bottoms, drunken MPs hugging colleagues who clearly didn't want to be hugged, members being 'helped' through the lobby by whips, or being propped up in case they collapsed in a drunken heap. In addition, whips heavily police the division lobby entrances and exits – and when there is a particularly sensitive issue at stake, emotions can run high. The same behaviour in a schoolyard or workplace would almost certainly see those involved suspended, yet we allow it in parliament. I have also seen members shouting at clerks and slamming their fists on the desk, furious about some perceived slight such as not knowing their name. Several clerks have told me they are delighted they are no longer needed in the division lobby thanks to the pass readers, because members engaged in such appalling behaviour. Of course, it's a tiny minority, but we all get tarred with the same brush.

My suggestion is simple. We should introduce cameras into the division lobbies. After all, the cameras in the chamber are recording during divisions and the result of a division (and how each MP voted) is public knowledge, so what are we hiding?

One final point about the building. In theory it is where the people can see democracy in action. In practice, it is remarkably difficult for the public to gain access. The queues for security are long, the building has terrible disabled access, the lighting is so dingy most people can't see where they are going, the charges for tours are extortionate, the ring of steel round the building is ugly, and parliamentary rigmarole renders most of our proceedings completely impenetrable. The whole place desperately needs a makeover. I don't just mean that we need to sort out the Victorian drains, Edwardian wiring and twentieth-century asbestos. The palace needs to become a physically welcoming place, looking less like an impregnable castle and reflecting openness, transparency and equality. Reactionary forces will be appalled, and we will almost certainly have to vacate the palace for a decade, if only because it will be far more expensive and risky to carry on sitting in a medieval building while it is being renovated and MPs will have to put up with considerable inconvenience. The alternatives for our temporary accommodation are limited as ministerial accountability requires parliament to sit close to the seat of government in Whitehall. Moreover the Palace of Westminster is part of a UNESCO World Heritage Site and an icon of democracy and of the rule of law, so suggestions that it should be done up and handed over to a hotel chain are wide of the mark. A basic minimum for both the temporary Commons and the restored palace would be full and open access for the public (as in the past and at the Bundestag) – and enough seats in the chamber for every MP (as in every other representative democracy).

To paraphrase Churchill,* since our buildings shape us, restoring the building and our democracy need to go hand in hand and the shilly-shallying and endless political meddling (which has so far seen many millions of pounds spent on Restoration and Renewal plans which have subsequently been torn up) has to end.

The Palace of Westminster (or 'Pestminster' if you read the tabloids) is a special place but it is not so special or unique that it cannot enter the modern era in its working practices. The old morality that condemned MPs for divorce, adultery and homosexuality was little better than the Old Corruption whereby seats and votes were sold. Both rested on hypocrisy. But parliament still needs a clear and unambiguous idea of what constitutes inappropriate behaviour. We can improve the support for MPs as employers and improve protections for staff, but the key lies in changing attitudes. Haughtiness, entitlement, arrogance, petulance and excessive informality need to be replaced by modern ideas of professionalism based on mutual respect. That won't be easy – but it is essential.

---

*Speaking of the reconstruction of the Commons after its wartime bombing, Churchill said, 'we shape our buildings and afterwards our buildings shape us.'

6

Conflict of Interest

Tuesday 1 May 2018. The Commons was debating the Sanctions and Anti-Money Laundering Bill. Not exactly riveting stuff, but really important if the UK is to tackle international criminality. A cross-party group of us, including Dame Margaret Hodge, Alison Thewliss and Sir Geoffrey Clifton-Brown, were trying to toughen up the Bill by insisting that the UK's overseas territories (OTs) like Gibraltar, the British Virgin, Cayman, and Turks and Caicos islands, which have long acted as tax havens, open up their financial systems to greater scrutiny. In particular, the former Tory chief whip Andrew Mitchell had tabled a new clause, which would force the OTs to have open, public registers of company interests. Sir Geoffrey Cox, the Conservative MP for Torridge and West Devon, asked one of my colleagues, Helen Goodman, who supported this amendment, 'What does the honourable Lady say to the 50,000 or 60,000 inhabitants of the Cayman Islands, who were given a constitution in which the responsibility for the governance of their financial and economic affairs was solemnly conveyed to them by this Parliament?' He later intervened on Margaret Hodge to say, 'In 2009, we gave the people of the Cayman Islands a solemn pledge in this House. We said, "We will not legislate for you in these areas of public responsibility without your consent." By this measure today, we are breaking that promise to them, and it is beneath the dignity of this Parliament to do away with that promise and that pledge of good faith.' These are perfectly reasonable points to make, but anticipating that a Labour MP was intending to ask the Speaker whether he should have declared an interest in the subject, Cox made a point of order saying, 'I have on occasions practised in some of the Caribbean countries that formed the basis of our discussion in my capacity as a member of the Bar.'[1] According to the register of financial interests, Messrs Travers, Thorp, Alberga, Attorneys, of Grand Cayman Island paid him £40,000 for sixty hours of work between September 2017 and February 2018 to advise private individuals.[2] He also went on to be instructed by the attorney general of the British Virgin Islands to advise her and all BVI government ministries in their ministerial capacities in a public commission of inquiry into 'serious dishonesty' of public officials in general in 2021 which concluded that, 'unless the most urgent and drastic steps are taken, the current unhappy situation – with elected officials deliberately ignoring the tenets of good governance giving rise to an environment in which the risks of dishonesty in relation to public decision-making and funding continue unabated – will go on indefinitely'.[3] So, Cox's knowledge and understanding of the OTs is extensive. Cox's position in respect of these matters is that no conflict of interest was involved when he spoke in the Commons, because the work he has done in the OTs 'had nothing whatsoever to do with the tax or financial policies of the Cayman Islands or any other jurisdiction but predominantly consisted of the defence of individuals against criminal charges of which they subsequently acquitted'.[4] He also makes the legitimate point that it is wrong to make a crude assimilation between a barrister and their client's cause or interests. While he agrees that his experience in the OTs has informed his view on how the UK should exercise its stewardship of the OTs, he has told me that he made his point of order out of an excess of caution, but that 'it was unnecessary, and because it has given rise to misconceived commentary ... I regret doing so.' However, while Cox maintains that no conflict of interest existed at the time of his remarks in the House, he has also said that he made the remarks about his experience in the OTs because the House has interpreted the duty of disclosure to arise even where no actual conflict exists. I believe he was right to do so, because the principle of openness dictates (and the Code of Conduct states) that an interest must be declared whenever 'those interests might reasonably be thought by others to influence his or her actions or words as a Member'.[5] If in any doubt, it is always better to declare a potential interest so the public can judge – and it is a self-evident fact that those with the most outside work are likely to have the most areas of potential conflict.

It's unquestionable that an MP should always resolve a conflict between their private interest and the public interest in the interests of the public. Yet issues like MPs' second jobs, inappropriate influence, lobbying and the role of APPGs, all-party parliamentary groups, remain unresolved, as we shall explore in this chapter.

SECOND JOBS

The mood has similarly vacillated in recent years on the question of MPs' 'second jobs'. Fifty years ago, it was considered A Good Thing for an MP to have an outside expertise and an alternative source of income. It meant they had something to offer and they were less open to bribes. But today many demand that all second jobs be banned. Thus Ipsos found in November 2021 that 52 per cent of the public disapprove of MPs being paid for second jobs and only 19 per cent approve.[6] Some of the criticism may be based in envy. It is understandable, especially in a time when most of our constituents are struggling with the cost-of-living crisis and depressed wages, that they were angry in January 2023 to see Sky News and Tortoise Media's league chart of MPs earning £17.2 million since the general election in 2019 in addition to their £86,584 salary. Theresa May's £2,550,876, Sir Geoffrey Cox's £2,191,387, Boris Johnson's £1,064,785, Fiona Bruce's £711,749 and John Redwood's £692,438 – or for that matter David Lammy's £202,599 – infuriate people.[*] Which is why the Labour MP Richard Burgon has introduced a ten-minute-rule bill aimed at stopping second jobs and Gordon Brown has recommended that the MPs' Code of Conduct 'should be strengthened with a general prohibition on second jobs by members of Parliament, with few exceptions for employment required to maintain professional memberships, such as medicine'.[7]

Some second jobs are evidently problematic, but if you are hoping that I too want to ban them all, I warn you that I am about to disappoint you. Let me explain. Some people, including a lot of Conservative MPs, claim that parliament is all the better for the number of MPs who

---

[*]These figures were correct at the time. In the first three months of 2023 Johnson registered a further £3,287,293.53 of outside earnings, Cox added £13,840, Bruce £111,428.04 and Lammy £18,847.

are actively engaged in other work. Jacob Rees-Mogg claims that it is 'an historic strength of our system, that MPs should have a wider focus than the Westminster bubble'.[8] That is not my argument.

My argument is threefold. Firstly, there is the time argument. I do not doubt the strength of public opinion on this. Ipsos found that 63 per cent of the public agree with the sentence 'MPs are paid to work full time for their constituents and to serve the country and they therefore should not have time to do other jobs as well.' In a similar vein, on the back of the Owen Paterson scandal, Boris Johnson suggested (and tabled a motion on 17 November 2021 to this effect) that the rules should be changed in line with a 2018 recommendation by the Committee on Standards in Public Life, which stated, 'The code of conduct for MPs should be updated to state that: any outside activity undertaken by an MP, whether remunerated or unremunerated, should be within reasonable limits and should not prevent them from fully carrying out their range of duties.'[9] In other words, the House of Commons should put a limit on the amount of time an MP can spend on any outside work (whether or not it is paid) or on the amount they are paid, so that every constituent can be assured that nothing is getting in the way of the MP fully carrying out their job. Johnson even wrote to the Speaker saying, 'adopting these specific recommendations would ensure that MPs who are neglecting their duties to their constituents and prioritising outside interests would be investigated, and appropriately punished by the existing disciplinary authorities'.[10] Leaving aside the fact that Mr Johnson's activities since leaving office, which have included repeatedly absenting himself from the Commons to make very well-paid speeches to corporate bodies, have not suggested that he embraced this principle as keenly as he advocated it for others, this *seems* sensible. An MP's outside activities should not so swamp their diary that they cannot 'fully carry out their range of duties'. I would go further. Being an MP is not just a full-time job. If done well, it's more than a full-time job. Most MPs work many more than forty hours a week. The public may only see the hours spent in the chamber, but when you add up select and public bill committees, APPGs, visits to local residents, businesses and charities, door-knocking sessions, surgeries, researching and writing speeches, dealing with complex casework, responding to emails, addressing outside conferences, travel to and from the constituency, attending countless internal party or caucus meetings, recruiting and managing staff, responding to media enquiries and appearing on radio and TV, the total comes closer to eighty or ninety hours a week. Most MPs work several hours every weekend. Yes, of course MPs have spare time. We'd go mad if we didn't carve it out. And I would argue that as long as an MP is assiduous and diligent in their duties, what spare time they have is their own.

The trouble is, how do you define any of these terms? How do you judge whether an MP is fully carrying out their range of (unspecified) duties? What would count as 'reasonable limits'? The government minister Ann-Marie Trevelyan suggested outside work should be limited to ten to twelve hours a week. I'm not sure many people would support that, if those hours were when the House is sitting, but what about someone who sleeps little and works from 4 until 8.30 every morning on writing a book, or analysing medical diagnostics, or buying and selling shares, or milking the cows? Is it enough for an MP to engage in 'parliamentary activities' (another wholly unspecified term) for forty hours a week, or sixty, or eighty?

We can all, however, spot when a colleague is swinging the lead. George Galloway may have thought he was engaging with a new audience when he joined the Big Brother House for three weeks in January 2006 (as a Respect Party MP), but his impression of a cat has been voted the cringiest reality TV moment of all time. The Labour chief whip Hilary Armstrong said at the time that he should 'respect his constituents, not his ego'.[11] But Nadine Dorries went one step further when she joined *I'm a Celebrity ... Get Me Out of Here!* in 2012. She claimed she was 'a bit of an anti-politician politician', that the show was a 'publicity gift' that enabled her to communicate directly with 16 million people and that it gave her a chance to 'big up Boris'. But she got into deeper water when she returned, as she was suspended from the Conservative Party and rebuked by the Standards Committee for refusing to declare her £82,000 fee on the basis that it had gone to her company Averbrook. The Committee quite rightly argued that it was wrong to use companies to avoid declaring sources of income and she was forced to apologise to the House (not before she had threatened to sue the commissioner for investigating her).[12] What is extraordinary is that she was readmitted to the Tory Party and later made a Cabinet minister. Equally appalling was Matt Hancock's decision to toddle off to the jungle for a month in 2022 when the House was sitting. He trotted out the same arguments as Dorries. People would get to see the real him. Politicians needed to engage with a wider public. None of it will have washed with his constituents or with the many people who lost loved ones to Covid, who see it as a squalid and unseemly attempt to carve an alternative career out of his

Covid prominence. It is difficult not to fume at his self-promotion – especially when it came with a £320,000 fee in the middle of a national cost-of-living crisis. The only rule change I can imagine that might put a stop to such gallivanting is the restoration of the rule instituted in 1801 but subsequently abolished that 'no member do presume to go out of town without leave of this House'. This rule also applied to attendance at committees. If the House nominated you, you had to attend. Thus when William Smith O'Brien refused to serve on a railway committee in 1846, the House had him detained overnight in the Clock Tower cell.* That might have helped Matt Hancock cool his heels.†

Despite these examples of manifestly inappropriate behaviour, there is also an inconvenient truth that, although there was an attempt to ban MPs from taking ministerial office (in 1713), it failed, and all ministers are expected to be a member of one or other House. Being a minister is an onerous second job. It limits an MP's freedom to represent their constituency, and it takes up a considerable amount of time. Ministers spend most of their day in their department or travelling, not in parliament, and in most cases it is also the highest paid of any second jobs held by MPs. Cabinet ministers in 2022–3 were entitled to an additional £72,454, ministers of state were on £34,742 and other junior ministers were on £24,947. That is why the Standards Committee declined to recommend a new rule

---

*The last person detained here was the founder of the National Secular Society Charles Bradlaugh when he refused to make a religious oath of allegiance as the new MP for Northampton in 1880. It is now used by the staff of the Petitions Committee.

†I have participated in one reality TV show, *Make Me Prime Minister*, on a Sunday in 2022. Four years earlier I turned down Kay Burley's offer to team up with her on *Hunted* (which would have raised money for charity) because there might be important votes in the Commons.

that would place a limit on the number of hours an MP spends on outside employment.

Secondly, drawing up a rule that says no MP can have any outside interest or income of whatever kind would be simple, but it would not be enforceable in a way that was fair or proportionate. By definition it would fail to catch some of the most egregious conflicts of interest, as it would apply only to paid employment rather than to unearned income. Moreover, the public has a more nuanced view than some might think. The same Ipsos poll found that a sizeable minority (41 per cent) agreed that if someone is doing 'a useful job helping others or benefitting the country, they shouldn't be expected to stop if they are elected as an MP'; 52 per cent approved of an MP working as a doctor for the NHS; and 50 per cent agreed with them being paid as an army reservist. What they really objected to was MPs being paid advisers to big businesses and multinational corporations. One significant step forward in this direction was taken recently when the House adopted the Standards Committee recommendation to introduce a ban on members providing paid parliamentary advice, consultancy or strategy services and requiring them to have a clear contract banning any paid lobbying. I worry that when the campaign group Led By Donkeys recently approached several MPs including Matt Hancock, Kwasi Kwarteng and Graham Brady about a possible consultancy role for a fake Korean company on £10,000 a day, Brady suggested that although he could not introduce anyone to ministers or officials as that would break the rules, he might be able to identify people in government to approach and 'how to do it in the most appropriate way'.[13] I am not a fan of these sting operations, which are effectively entrapment, and none of the three MPs ever took up the employment, but Brady's understanding flies in the face of advice from the commissioner: 'Giving advice as to how an employer might achieve a particular objective in relation to a particular legislative provision or other matter departs from the general for the specific, and would be likely to amount to a breach of paragraph 9 of the Code.'[14]

A more extensive limit on paid employment where there is potential for a conflict of interest now makes sense, albeit with the kind of exceptions I have already listed. Nearly everyone who suggests exemptions to such a rule, including Gordon Brown, mentions medicine. Richard Burgon's Members of Parliament (Prohibition of Second Jobs) Bill has an even wider exemption for 'employment in the NHS, social care or emergency services, or where it is necessary to maintain existing professional qualifications'. I agree. Nobody wants to stop a nurse such as Maria Caulfield, a dentist like Sir Paul Beresford or a doctor like Rosena Allin-Khan or Dan Poulter from continuing to practise. This is not just because they need to keep their eye in and maintain their professional qualifications. Their frontline experience in the NHS is useful in parliament, they perform a public service and they are sorely needed. But the same could be argued for a farmer, or a human rights lawyer. Keir Starmer has also argued that broadcasting, speechmaking and writing articles and books are extensions of politics and a legitimate aspect of being an MP, even when remunerated. He has a point. If we had banned MPs from writing books or articles (I know I'm not exactly disinterested) or if we insisted that MPs cannot be paid for them, we would never have had important volumes like Anthony Crosland's *The Future of Socialism* (which was mostly written before he lost his seat), or the journalism of Michael Foot and George Lansbury, or Winston Churchill's *History of the*

English-Speaking Peoples. We might have been able to live without some of the novels MPs have written, but a total ban on writing would have deprived us of the published diaries of Barbara Castle, Alan Clarke and Tony Benn. Who is to say that a farmer running a family agricultural business in a rural constituency is not the perfect person to represent that seat? And why should we demand that any such person immediately relinquish their farming business or close it down on election? I also think that it is useful to have some MPs who are also councillors (or even council leaders, like Ben Bradley who is MP for Mansfield and leader of Nottinghamshire County Council), as most public services in the UK are delivered not by parliament but by councils, so having an up-to-date understanding of the pressures they face is useful and there is no conflict of interest.

Some have suggested that the rule should be clear but should have a limited number of exemptions. Here is my suggestion:

No member of parliament shall accept payment or remuneration for any outside employment other than:

- Ministerial office
- Elected office as a town, borough or county councillor
- Working as a clinician in or for the NHS, a special constable, a fire officer or a reservist in the armed forces
- Performing a public service as a chartered regulator
- Maintaining a professional qualification or a family business
- Exercising their freedom of speech and expression as an author, broadcaster, actor, musician, publisher or speaker

Thirdly – and this is my main point – the above suggestions would go some way to addressing the perceived problem, but they would not affect the highest outside earners such as Johnson; and the real issue about second jobs, or any outside financial interest, is the potential conflict of interest. The only possible conflict of interest that could arise from an MP doing a night shift in their local A&E every week is if they were to lobby parliament, ministers or officials for additional funding for their hospital or department, or to keep the A&E open. By contrast, it is all too easy to see a potential conflict were an MP to take a job as a strategic adviser, director or political consultant. That is where the fault line still lies.

LOBBYING

Lobbying is a quintessential aspect of politics and any attempt to suggest otherwise is as silly as fishermen complaining about the swell of the sea. Indeed, the French president Jacques Chirac sounded petty when he complained that the UK had won the Olympics for London in 2005 only because of Tony Blair's personal 'lobbying' of the IOC. Besides, the very word 'lobbying' (in English, French and Spanish) comes from Westminster, as the old chamber of the House of Commons, the former St Stephen's Chapel, consisted of a two-storey building whose upper floor had a long thin chapel with benches facing inwards ranged in three bays, divided from a 'lobby' consisting of two further bays. Only MPs could enter the chapel/chamber, but it was considered a fundamental aspect of representative democracy that members of the public could loiter in the lobby hoping to catch their MP and bend their ear. When parliament burnt down in 1834, the old lobby was replaced with a larger octagonal Central Lobby halfway between the Lords and the Commons, where any member of the public can turn up and demand to see their MP. Thanks to other modes of access to MPs, this freedom is used less frequently today, but when I was first elected in 2001 doorkeepers would come in search of MPs wherever we were in the building, and if they tracked us down we were expected to go and find our constituent and hear them out.

Lobbying is also a valuable part of the system. Take the Mental Health Act 2007. I sat on the Bill Committee when it was going through the Commons. I had no medical expertise, but I wanted to ensure the Bill achieved a proper balance between protecting the public and safeguarding the rights of patients with mental health conditions including personality disorders (this balance was and remains a controversial matter). Far from hiding from lobbyists, I invited them in. I listened to mental health charities, patients' groups, the British Medical Association, pharmaceutical companies and clinicians. I made my own mind up about what was the right thing to do, but I tried to garner the evidence beforehand – and that meant talking to lobbyists. The legislation is now ripe for reform, but the amendments that I tabled improved the government's Bill. That would not have happened without lobbying.

The art, therefore, it to weed out corrupt lobbying – that is, based on preferential access or inappropriate influence. The Commons has forbidden such 'paid lobbying' ever since two tawdry incidents in 1695. The first related to the East India Company, which had set aside a whopping £90,000 to bribe MPs in the hope of obtaining a new parliamentary charter. Eleven MPs were involved, including the famously cross-eyed Speaker, Sir John Trevor,[15] plus Thomas Osborne, the recently created duke of Leeds, who was lord president of the Council and was said to have received nearly £6,000. He denied it, but then tried to return the money, thereby manifestly undermining his denial. Two parliamentary inquiries led to the impeachment of the duke followed by a Commons motion declaring that 'the offer of money, or other advantage, to any Member of Parliament for the promoting of any matter whatsoever, depending or to be transacted in Parliament, is a high crime and misdemeanour and tends to the subversion of the English constitution'.[16] By some extraordinary sleight of hand, although Sir Thomas Cooke and Sir Basil Firebrace were briefly imprisoned in the Tower, none of those implicated were expelled or suspended from parliament. However, the new motion proved problematic later that year when the Orphans Bill was enacted. The City of London Corporation, which outrageously wanted to continue raiding various charitable funds to alleviate the its own financial difficulties, was heavily promoting this controversial measure. When the Commons learnt that John Hungerford, the chairman of Ways and Means (i.e. the principal Deputy Speaker), who presided over the committee stage, had received a 'gratuity' of twenty guineas, and that Sir John Trevor had allowed a thousand guineas to cross his sweaty palm, all to help the smooth passage of the Bill, the Commons invoked the new rule and duly expelled both men.

Almost exactly 300 years later the cash-for-questions scandal brought paid lobbying back into the limelight, when a sting operation by the *Sunday Times* in July 1994 revealed that two Conservative MPs, Graham

Riddick and David Tredinnick, had each accepted a £1,000 payment to table a parliamentary question. One might have expected any MP with half a brain to have been put on the alert by this, but three months later a very similar scandal came to light, when the *Guardian* revealed that two other Conservative MPs, Tim Smith and Neil Hamilton, had accepted payments from the lobbyist Ian Greer on behalf of Mohamed al-Fayed, the owner of Harrods, to table parliamentary questions, at the inflated price of £2,000 apiece. The government was stung into action. It set up the Nolan Committee, which recommended that a new post of parliamentary commissioner for standards be created, along with a ten-member Committee of Standards and Privileges, which should consider MPs' conduct and draft the first Code of Conduct for members.

In the meantime, the House had to consider the matter of Riddick and Tredinnick, on the back of a report by the old-style Committee of Privileges. Yet again it felt as if MPs were in denial. The Committee recommended on 4 April 1995 that they be suspended for ten and twenty days respectively, but lots of MPs simply refused to take the matter seriously. Julian Brazier tabled an amendment that would have limited their sanction to a mere reprimand; and 156 MPs, including twenty government ministers, wrote to Riddick's constituency association declaring their confidence in his 'honesty and propriety'. Only two men seemed truly shocked: the Labour MP Kevin Barron, who wanted the two men permanently expelled, and John Biffen, the former leader of the Commons, who suggested that the men's behaviour went 'to the very heart of what are proper relationships and conduct in this House of Commons'.[17] Nolan's recommendations were implemented soon afterwards and as soon as

Sir Michael Downey was appointed as commissioner, he started an investigation into twenty-five MPs who al-Fayed alleged had been involved with Ian Greer. In the end, the electoral timetable trammelled up events, as the commissioner's report was not published until after the general election in 1997. Downey exonerated twenty MPs, but criticised four, namely Michael Brown, Sir Andrew Bowden, Sir Michael Grylls and Tim Smith. The Standards and Privileges Committee concluded in relation to each that 'if he were still a Member, we would recommend a period of suspension from the service of the House'. In Grylls' case they added that they would have recommended a 'substantial period of suspension ... augmented to take account of his deceit'.[18] This just left the appallingly incorrigible Neil Hamilton, who had been heavily defeated in his supposedly safe seat of Tatton by the BBC journalist turned anti-corruption candidate Martin Bell.

This may feel like ancient history, but it is instructive. You can attribute the collapse of the Major government in 1997 to many things, but the cash-for-questions scandal played an important part because it exposed a fundamental abuse of trust (and a sense of entitlement) by ruling politicians. My concern is that the same is true today, because we still haven't properly sorted out our act.

For a start, paid lobbying is not, by definition, a one-man show. You can't, as it were, lobby yourself. Owen Paterson was peddling influence for his clients, just like Hamilton and Grylls, but ministers, including Priti Patel, Matt Hancock, Lord Bethell and Rory Stewart were happy to deal with Paterson, even though they could and should have known that he had a direct financial interest. They claimed there was nothing untoward and that their civil servants would have told them if there was, but each of Paterson's meetings and approaches constituted paid lobbying. So, just as in the 1990s, the primary culprit, the lobbyist, was sanctioned, but the ministers who'd been lobbied evaded any criticism (and effectively colluded by trooping through the lobby to defend Paterson). Both sides may not be equally culpable, but we will never put an end to paid lobbying unless ministers are more alert to the rules.

This is still a live issue. The House of Lords recently suspended two members, the Conservative earl of Shrewsbury and the Labour life peer Baroness Goudie, for nine and six months respectively, for paid lobbying – yet the ministers they lobbied faced no censure at all. Although these suspensions are longer than most Commons suspensions, unlike an MP neither of them can face a recall petition, and both retain their seat for life – another indictment of the capricious nature of parliamentary justice. This takes me to a subsidiary point. The Recall of MPs Act has an unintended effect on how the Standards Committee views potential sanctions, as we are conscious that any suspension of more than ten days is in effect handing the MP over to the mercy of their constituents – and is likely to lead to them losing their job. The tendency is therefore to hand down shorter suspensions. The Committee can, if it wants, suspend an MP for less than ten days while simultaneously withdrawing their pay for a longer period. But some breaches of the code are serious enough to warrant a month's suspension, though not quite so serious as to invoke the Act. The danger is that the House is left with little choice – either a brief suspension or what is tantamount to expulsion. That makes the Commons seem feeble. I would therefore now amend the Act so that the Committee on Standards can recommend a longer suspension without necessarily invoking the Act, while giving it the power to invoke the Act if it thinks it appropriate. I am also conscious that the Act is more perilous for MPs in marginal constituencies, which is yet another reason why it might be more impactful on an individual MP to suspend them for three or six months rather than ten days.

David Cameron once predicted that 'the far-too-cosy relationship between politics and money' was 'the next big scandal waiting to happen'.[19] This was obviously before he became an adviser and lobbyist for the supply-chain financing company Greensill. He was right, though. A few simple changes are now necessary to clean up lobbying. Firstly, we should extend the scope of the Lobbying Act,[*] which at present covers only consultant lobbyists, to include in-house lobbyists such as those who work for multinational companies like Greensill. Secondly, the Cabinet Office should publish a monthly list of all contacts with ministers where a matter is raised that has a bearing on official business or where an attempt is made to influence a public policy decision. This should include meetings with MPs, together with details of the subjects covered (and whether or not a financial interest was declared). And thirdly, we should bar MPs from receiving gifts or hospitality above the legal £1,500 threshold from a person or organisation deemed to be an 'impermissible donor' under the Political Parties, Elections and Referendums Act 2000.

---

[*] Its formal title is the Transparency of Lobbying, Non-party Campaigning and Trade Union Administration Act of 2014.

ALL-PARTY PARLIAMENTARY GROUPS

Parliament also has a soft underbelly when it comes to inappropriate lobbying, in the form of all-party parliamentary groups (APPGs). These are informal bicameral groups (that is, of both Houses), which are allowed to use parliamentary facilities and the crowned portcullis APPG logo if they abide by a loose set of rules. The problem is, there are now more than 780 APPGs (more than there are MPs), the register runs to 1,369 pages, the rules are full of holes, the quorum for an AGM is just five, and although details have to be registered they are subject to very little scrutiny. In addition, because there are no parliamentary staff or resources to run these groups, they depend either on the capacity of the lead MP's office to take on the extra work or on an external secretariat. Many APPGs are run entirely out of an MP's office, with no financial support at all. But the amount of money involved can be considerable. In this parliament, the Fair Business Banking APPG has received £571,500 in benefits in kind and in cash; the Anti-Corruption and Responsible Tax APPG has received £334,500; the Carbon Monoxide APPG (of which I am a vice-chair) has received £295,500. Nearly all of this comes in the shape of benefits in kind, i.e. staff time organising meetings and printing materials.

In the main APPGs are A Good Thing. They enable subjects that might otherwise be ignored to get public attention and traction in parliament. The Acquired Brain Injury APPG, which I set up with support from the UK Acquired Brain Injury Forum, has already led to significant changes in how brain injury is dealt with in prisons and in sport. There are groups on Ending Homelessness, Cancer, Cardiac Risk in the Young,

Carers, Cats, Dog Advisory Welfare, Park Homes, Parkrun and Parkinson's, Children, Children in Police Custody, Children of Alcoholics and Children who need Palliative Care. I cannot fault any one of these. However, there is duplication. Crispin Blunt, for instance, chairs the Cannabidoil Products group (secretariat courtesy of Tenacious Labs), while Tonia Antoniazzi chairs the Medical Cannabis under Prescription group. There are Media, Media Freedom and Media Literacy groups. There is a Caribbean group, an Overseas Territories group and a group for each Caribbean country and each Overseas Territory. And there are nine cancer groups.

Sometimes, the impetus and drive for an APPG comes from an external body, an industry body, a company or a lobbying or public relations firm. The secretariat for the Business Travel APPG is provided by the Business Travel Association; Channel 4 provides it for the Channel 4 APPG; Macmillan Cancer Support does the same for the Cancer group. (I could go on.) This too is often completely innocuous. Many groups have no income and no (or next to no) external support. They simply enable a few MPs and peers to meet together and pursue an interest. Hundreds register a few thousand pounds for the cost of a staff member working a day a month. They often feel like the beating heart of Westminster, as their informality allows cross-party working in a way that defies most of the stereotypes about parliament and they give charities access to the parliamentary system. Of course, therefore, the Spinal Injuries Association supports its group (to the tune of £1,500 to £3,000 a year) and the Stroke Association supports its group (£3,001 to £4,500).

In some instances, the connection is via a consultancy. The Business Resilience APPG, whose declared aim is 'to focus on macro issues affecting businesses in the

UK to ensure that we are commercially resilient', is supported by Wychwood Consulting, which is in turn paid by Cignpost Diagnostics Ltd, which says it delivers 'business continuity and assurance through empowering people to take control of their health outcomes'.[20]

Some firms run multiple APPGs. The 'cross-party think tank' Policy Connect funds APPGs on Carbon Monoxide, Health, Assistive Technology, Climate Change, Sustainable Resource, Data Analytics, Design and Innovation, and Skills and Employment – and states that it specialises in 'supporting parliamentary groups'. By January 2023 it had contributed £1,627,526 in benefits in kind to APPGs in this parliament. Connect Communications had supported fourteen APPGs to the tune of £981,037, including £193,000 for the Hydrogen APPG. Healthcomms Consulting had supported nine, including Adult Social Care, Vascular and Venous Disease, Obesity and Women's Health, at a cost of £708,000. It describes itself as 'an award-winning healthcare communications agency, specialising in public affairs, market access and media relations', but it is owned by Political Lobbying & Media Relations Limited, and one of its former directors is Paul Bristow MP. Similarly, College Green Group has contributed £636,000 to four APPGs, including £307,000 to the Housing Market and Housing Delivery APPG. It boasts, 'We function as the Secretariat to a range of All-Party Parliamentary Groups, allowing for cross-party, issue-based problem solving, with high-level activity and management.'[21] Its sole director is Thomas Borwick, the son of a Conservative hereditary peer and the former MP for Kensington, who was the chief technology officer for Vote Leave and worked for Cambridge Analytica. Tendo Consulting ('your

public affairs, communications and campaigns agency')
has provided £255,000 for seven groups, including
the Future of Aviation, Road Freight and Logistics,
Air Passenger Duty Reform, Medical Cannabis under
Prescription and Pharmacy (£139,000).[22]

This may be innocent, but it is opaque. These
companies are not doing this work out of the goodness
of their hearts. It is reasonable to presume that they have
clients who pay them to do this work – and expect results.
Yet those clients – the real paymasters – remain hidden
from view. APPGs seem to have become part of these
companies' standard operating practice and their business
plan. This is wrong – and it needs reform. We could either
ban APPGs from receiving more than a certain level of
support from any outside source – perhaps £1,500 per
annum – or we could prohibit anyone registered as a
consultant lobbyist (which would include all the above
firms) from providing the secretariat for an APPG.

We also need to tighten the rules. As things stand, the
quorum is just five and I cannot tell you how often the
cry has gone up 'Is anyone free for two minutes to pop
into such and such room to help us form a quorum?' I get
why we do it, but it does raise the question of whether
a group that cannot muster five members out of the 650
MPs and 780 peers really has the necessary support to
consider itself an all-party parliamentary group rather
than just an informal ginger group. That is why for any
APPG that receives outside assistance in cash or in kind
I would require the following at an AGM: a quorum
of eight, a list of twenty active members, a statement of
accounts and activities, an external chair appointed by
the Speaker, the appointment of four officers (at least
one of whom should be from the government, one
Opposition and one peer) who are equally and severally

responsible for the financial and proper conduct of the group, and the publication of the ultimate funding of the group (such as a PR company's clients).*

As Boris Johnson has shown time and again, it is easy to acquit yourself in the court of your own opinion, and MPs often plead all manner of excuses for their conflation of the public interest with their own. Owen Paterson repeatedly claimed that he was only bringing a matter of serious danger to ministers' attention as he peddled influence around Whitehall on behalf of his paying clients. But we should be utterly ruthless with ourselves – and expect the public to be ruthless with us if we get it wrong. Of course it is always easier to see the mote in another's eye than the plank in one's own, but MPs' inability to see when they have confused their own private interest with the public interest is a very special form of blindness. I especially despair when colleagues are caught in journalists' sting operations, as befell Sir Graham Brady, Matt Hancock, Kwasi Kwarteng and Scott Benton – and I believe it is time we introduced a new rule forbidding MPs from *offering* to provide privileged access to parliament, table questions or leak a report for financial reward, regardless of whether or not a client ever takes up that offer or money changes hands. As I've said several times already, MPs don't have to be saints. But we have to change the culture of entitlement, bolster the concept of genuine public service and strengthen the rules so that public service is at the heart of everything we do, and we need to do so now.

---

*These proposals were included in the Standards Committee report on APPGs in April 2023 but at the time of writing they have yet to be adopted.

7

Helping Ourselves

The first motion I tabled as an MP in 2001 called for parliamentary reform. To be precise, it expressed a desire for a 'wholly or substantially elected second chamber'. Twenty years later I think the need for reform is greater than ever. The way people talk of the 'Great' Reform Act of 1832, you would think it snatched Britain out of its swampy past on to the highlands of electoral purity in one fell swoop, but in truth parliamentary reform was the result of decades of separate measures. The secret ballot was only introduced in 1872, corrupt electoral practices were not outlawed until 1883 and universal adult suffrage was not in place until 1930. So too, we have tackled parliamentary corruption piecemeal down the ages, which is why we have such a complex patchwork of regulatory bodies and codes of conduct.

It is time that changed. We urgently need a sustained programme of parliamentary reform, covering every aspect of standards in parliament. Why? Because good government is not about ruling the roost, it is about changing the world for the better. It depends on consent freely given, and that in turn depends on trust. When parliamentary standards fall – or when parliament makes itself incomprehensible – trust wears thin. When people assume politicians lie, politicians presume they might as well lie – and so we spiral into the drain. Those of us who believe that our nation can prosper and that a fairer, better society is possible need people to believe in the power of the ballot box and trust that parliament does what it says on the tin, that it enables debate, that it represents the best of people and that it conducts its business without fear or favour.

I have offered several suggestions throughout the book of important changes we should make. Some of these reforms require alterations to our standing orders; others need new laws. All require political will – and will undoubtedly face opposition – but I believe they are vital for the reinvigoration and survival of parliament and representative democracy. They are as follows:

- We should end the government's exclusive control of the Commons order paper and timetable, handing it over to a cross-party Business Committee, elected by the whole House, which would consider and propose the future business of the House, guarantee time for government and private members' legislation and ensure enough time is allocated for all important or controversial legislation.
- In addition to the annual Budget statement and instead of the archaic estimates system for agreeing government spending, the chancellor of the Exchequer should present an annual statement of government accounts and all members should be allowed to table amendments to it, so that income and expenditure are agreed by parliament. Members would also be able to table suggestions to increase or cut the police and local government grants and annual benefits upratings.

- To ensure that parliament is a safe place for anyone to work or visit, the House should introduce a system for suspending MPs as a neutral act pending investigation where an MP has been arrested or charged with a serious sexual or violent crime.
- To clean up lobbying in parliament, there should be new, tougher rules on APPGs, MPs should be banned from taking second jobs apart from a short list of exemptions and all ministerial financial interests should be registered with the Commons or Lords registrar of financial interests and published within a fortnight of appointment. Ministers should also publish all meetings, hospitality, gifts and travel every month.
- The government should also introduce a new Parliamentary Standards Reform Bill which would amalgamate the independent adviser on ministers' interests, the Advisory Committee on Business Appointments and the House of Commons and House of Lords' commissioners for standards into a single independent national commissioner for ethics and standards, accountable to parliament, and bring the Commons Code of Conduct, the Lords rules, the Behaviour Code and the Ministerial Code together into a single parliamentary code. It should also require Commons support for any proposal to suspend, prorogue or adjourn parliament (either overnight or for a longer period) and to dissolve it for an early general election and end the practice of secondary legislation coming into force before it is published or has been considered by parliament.
- A Recall and Resignation of MPs Bill would end the ludicrous requirement for an MP to apply for an 'office of profit' such as the Chiltern Hundreds

in order to resign and enable MPs to resign by simply writing to the Speaker. It should also clarify the Recall of MPs Act 2015 to allow the Commons to determine if and when the Act is invoked.

- I would also introduce two new offences: knowingly, intentionally or recklessly misleading parliament as a government minister and refusing to correct the record when required to do so by the Office for National Statistics or the national commissioner for ethics and standards; and refusing to give evidence once legitimately summoned to a parliamentary committee of inquiry.

- I would also like to see a separate bill to reform the composition and powers of the second chamber, ending jobs for life in the legislature, separating the honours system from a seat in parliament, cutting the number to 180 and electing a third of them at each general election on a proportional regional system. In the meantime, the House of Lords Appointments Commissions should have the statutory power to refuse a nomination to the Lords.

CHANGING ATTITUDES

Changing parliamentary processes will not suffice, though. MPs' attitudes and behaviour also need a radical renovation if we are to regain public trust. I was sharply reminded of this when I was about to board a train at Paddington station on my way back to the Rhondda from parliament and I heard someone randomly shout 'terrible MP'. It wasn't clear whether the person meant me or someone else, but the problem of MPs' low standing is acute.

It set me thinking. We have been our own worst enemies at times. The expenses saga compounded the impression that we are all interested only in feathering our own nest. I include myself in this. I made a stupid mistake, for instance, when the government recalled parliament, very unusually, on a Saturday in October 2019. Conscious that some of my colleagues had childcare responsibilities, I asked that the Commons nursery be opened or that MPs be reimbursed. Social media – and many of my constituents – understandably went wild. People were already fed up with the gridlocked parliament failing to come to a resolution on Brexit, many families were struggling to pay for their own childcare and here was a well-paid MP apparently demanding extra financial support just for turning up for work on a Saturday. Many also incorrectly thought I had children. Indeed the 'Tripe Marketing Board' wittily set up a crowdfunder page saying, 'Chris Bryant is a struggling MP representing the Rhondda – one of the poorest parts of the UK. Can you help him with childcare costs?' It raised £604, all of which went to a children's charity called Kind.

The language we use about each other often lets us down, too. I don't mind a well-crafted political insult, but too much of today's verbal jousting is just cheap and nasty. The exorbitant language of 'scum', 'traitor', 'quisling', 'lynch' and 'bitch' should never be part of the lexicon of politics. Political opponents are not enemies, let alone 'enemies of the state'. The Privileges Committee is not a 'kangaroo court'. If we expend all our energy on throwing mud, not one of us will be clean – and if we constantly drip toxin into the well, we shall all be poisoned. A little magnanimity goes a long way, and voters prefer to see us working for the common endeavour rather than trying to take lumps out of each other.

We're also terrible at explaining what we do, so nobody really knows what the job of an MP entails. Some people seem to think we should sit in the chamber every moment that the House sits. Others think we should never leave our constituency and should act as an alternative social service. I have had emails from constituents demanding that I sort out the Christmas tree in Treorchy 'which is on the wonk'; and asking what to do with some chicks that had been dumped on a local doorstep. Most MPs' staff spend their time entirely on casework, reporting potholes or faulty street lights, arranging drain inspections, chasing down medical appointments, trying to sort people's housing or making representations to energy companies, the Home Office or the police. Covid added to this workload enormously, as government intervened so directly in people's lives during the pandemic that constituents got used to asking for advice from the closest thing to a government representative, their MP. My office dealt with 3,997 cases raised by my constituents last year. They included requests for information or advice, complaints about local services and appeals for assistance. Some were easily resolved. Others took many hours and months for a satisfactory outcome. In a few cases (such as complaints about the outcome of a trial) there was nothing I could do to help. I don't underestimate this role as chief local advocate. It is the basic bread and butter of the job. Sometimes the magic letters 'MP' have a surprising affect. When Kerry Foods was suing a Rhondda company for trading as 'Mr Creemy' and selling ice cream under that name (as it had done long before Kerry Foods trademarked its own 'Mr Creemy', but without legal protection), I rang the office of the chairman of Kerry Foods with little hope of getting through, but was amazed that he rang me back in minutes – and swiftly agreed to suspend the legal action as the Rhondda firm was now called Subzero.

But in truth I feel we MPs have lost our way – and in the process lost confidence in our core function. Our role as a constituency MP, listening to constituents, addressing their concerns, fighting their corner, is the bedrock of what we do, but in the old days an MP saw their primary role as helping to govern the nation and holding the powerful to account. They got elected and went to Westminster to exercise their judgement on behalf of their constituents on the matters of the day. As Edmund Burke put it (p. 140), 'It is [an MP's] duty to sacrifice his repose, his pleasures, his satisfactions, to [his constituents]; and above all, ever, and in all cases, to prefer their interest to his own. But his unbiassed opinion, his mature judgment, his enlightened conscience, he ought not to sacrifice to you, to any man, or to any set of men living.' He added 'a flatterer you do not wish for'. But today, as the broadcaster John Humphrys has argued,

> Their first role, as many MPs see it, is to be in their constituencies rather than in Westminster, dealing with their constituents' problems at their surgeries. It's a role encouraged by their parties as the safest way for them to retain their seats. And, for the same reason, they need to achieve as high a profile as they can. Now more than ever that means on social media where they are obliged constantly to tweet their views on each and every subject, however banal those views might be.[1]

I was struck, in the aftermath of the horrific murder of Sir David Amess in 2021, that many people commented online and in the media that he was different from the rest, because he was such an assiduous 'constituency MP'. It is true that he spoke up for his community whenever he had a chance, but he also took his parliamentary duties seriously, often fulfilling the dull but necessary job of chairing public bill committees. He certainly never saw constituency work as better or more important than proper scrutiny of legislation and of government. To my mind, a truly great MP keeps those two elements in balance – the constituency and the nation – so neither excludes the other.

Many of our greatest – and most respected – politicians rarely ventured into their constituency. No MP could get away with that for long today. But today's and tomorrow's MPs need to find a route back to statesmanship, rather than endlessly fretting about our latest clip for Facebook or Twitter. A sustained, nuanced, well-argued ten-minute speech is probably better, more useful, more effective, more important than a three-minute contribution full of headlines and soundbites (sound and fury) but no substance (signifying nothing). Expertise is more important than rent-a-quotism. And perhaps MPs' singular concentration on the local aspects of the job to the detriment of their national leadership role has helped breed the contempt in which they are held, because many have become little more than flatterers. After all, it may seem counter-intuitive, but most polling suggests that voters think we should put the nation before our local patch.

GOOD ENOUGH MPS

In the end, parliament will only ever be as respected as its members enable it to be. A Good Enough Parliament will need good enough MPs.

I'm not the first to say this. My witty, eager, principled and clever former Welsh colleague Paul Flynn, who died in 2019 after nearly thirty-two years as the MP for Newport West, was especially proud of having spent nearly all his time in parliament on the backbenches. But in July 2016 nearly all Jeremy Corbyn's Shadow Cabinet resigned – including me – and Jeremy appointed Paul as my temporary replacement as shadow leader of the House. Paul was eighty and joked that his arrival at the despatch box would improve the diversity of a parliament whose front benches suffered from a 'a total absence of octogenarians'.[2] He was equally jocular when Corbyn replaced him three months later. 'Our glorious leader,' he said, 'in an act of pioneering diversity, courageously decided to give opportunities for geriatrics on the front bench and this was so successful that he decided to create opportunities for geriatrics on the back bench. I'm doubly blessed.'[3] Paul also wrote the best guidebook to being an MP, *Commons Knowledge: How to Be a Backbencher*, which was first published in 1997 and updated as *How to Be an MP* in 2012.

Recognising that it 'will take many years to rebuild trust in politics', especially after the expenses scandal, Paul urged all MPs to 'abide by the Backbenchers' Ten Commandments'. These included wise saws like 'understate promises, never exaggerate successes', 'avoid serving commercial or partial interests' and 'admit failures'. Paul set high standards and was deeply sceptical about ministerial office. He (to my mind, rightly) wanted to shift power from the executive to the legislature. Hence his emphasis on the importance of backbench MPs. I too have spent most of my years on the backbenches and am passionate to see the House of Commons take back control from government. But the role of MPs is not just to scrutinise government, but also to staff and sustain it, and to enable it to govern effectively. So my version of what a good enough MP looks like applies equally to those who seek and to those who eschew a ministerial career.

The real difference will only come when MPs embrace high standards of conduct for themselves. I don't pretend this is easy. I know I will continue to make poor decisions. But we have to try. Yes, of course, we MPs are flawed. Our motives are not always pure. We can be vain, narcissistic, arrogant and proud. Some of us don't just have feet of clay, like the fatally flawed statue of King Nebuchadnezzar in the Book of Daniel; we are clay from head to toe. A few MPs have so little self-awareness or capacity to feel shame that they should never have been selected by their party, let alone sailed into parliament on their party's rising tide. We have a fair number of thugs, too. Sometimes we over-egg the pudding and we exaggerate for effect. But in that we are no different from the rest of humanity. We humans are neither wholly good nor wholly bad, but streaky. We veer drunkenly between generosity and jealousy, magnanimity and asperity. Sometimes we do the right thing but for the wrong reason – and vice versa. We might have to tell a lie to protect a greater good. Even saints can suffer from overweening vanity, pride and ambition.

But a good enough MP tries to provide leadership within parliament, their community, their party and the country. They value their role as a backbench MP as much as any time they spend as a minister and take the scrutiny of legislation as seriously from the government benches as in opposition. They cooperate with others – including in other political parties – to achieve change that can improve people's lives, promote our national prosperity or enhance our international standing. They have a proper, but never sycophantic or narcissistic, regard for the media and for those in senior office. They use the gift of the gab to expose the truth, not to obscure it. They are diligent in helping constituents, and never make promises they can't keep. They are prepared to surrender high office on a point of principle, but rarely threaten to resign out of self-righteous pride or in a fit of pique. They keep in balance the competing demands of family and of work, and of private and public life. They pursue policies based on evidence rather than search for evidence to confirm their prejudices and preconceptions. They are as magnanimous in defeat as in victory. They always check themselves for hypocrisy, sanctimony, excessive partisanship and conflicts of interest. And perhaps above all they retain a sense of humour – and proportion.

I end with two pleas. Firstly, if you are frustrated by what you see going on in parliament – or, for that matter, by this book – don't just shout at the television or the page, get involved. Join a party, make a fuss, clamour for change, put yourself up for election. Parliament needs you. My second plea is to my colleagues and is based on what the leader of the Opposition Harold Wilson said in 1963, the day after John Profumo had resigned as a minister for having lied to parliament. 'The sickness', he said, 'of an unrepresentative sector of our society should not detract from the robust ability of our people as a whole to face the challenge of the future. And in preparing to face that challenge, let us frankly recognise that the inspiration and the leadership must come first here in this House.'[4] Leadership is the most important of the Nolan Principles – and we MPs are called to lead. These last few years have undoubtedly found us wanting.

There is a lot of followership – following political trends, jumping on bandwagons, lending support for fashionable campaigns. Some of the leadership on offer has led us into a very dark place, too, where standards in public life are treated at best as an irritant. But we are an immensely resourceful nation, well served by our scepticism of demagogues. And change is always possible. There is a generation of politicians coming through who are sassy, intelligent, hard-working and inspirational. I won't name them. You can spot them. And perhaps you'll join their ranks.

Parliament's Regulatory Bodies

Each of the two Houses of Parliament has a Code of Conduct, which governs the registration and declaration of outside financial interests such as outside employment, gifts and hospitality, the use of parliamentary facilities, the rules on paid lobbying and the general expectations of members. This includes, in the Commons, a catch-all provision that 'Members shall never undertake any action which would cause significant damage to the reputation and integrity of the House of Commons as a whole, or of its Members generally.' The Code is enforced in the Commons by the parliamentary commissioner for standards, who alone initiates investigations into alleged breaches, either on their own initiative, on the back of a complaint or on a member's self-referral. If the commissioner considers there has been a substantive breach, they report it to the Committee on Standards, which has seven MPs (in party-political proportion to the members of the House) and seven lay members appointed after an open competition by the House of Commons Commission, the statutory body chaired by the Speaker which runs the Commons. If the Committee agrees that there has been a breach, it can recommend a sanction to the House such as an apology in a personal statement on the floor of the House, a temporary suspension (with loss of income) or permanent expulsion. Suspension and expulsion require a vote in the Commons, which means the government has to make time for it, by convention as soon as possible. A member can appeal against an adverse decision of the Standards Committee (and any sanction it proposes) to the Independent Expert Panel (see below), but the House takes any final decision on suspension or expulsion on a motion without debate or amendment. The process is encapsulated in the Procedural Protocol, which lays down what any MP can expect during an investigation.

The Privileges Committee (which normally constitutes the same seven MPs as the Standards Committee) is able to consider only matters of privilege (such as a witness refusing to appear before a committee of the House, or a member or witness misleading the House) that have been referred to it by the House of Commons. It can recommend sanctions, which are considered on an amendable and votable motion by the whole House.

Both Houses have also agreed a Behaviour Code and are signed up to the Independent Complaints and Grievance Scheme, which mounts confidential investigations into complaints and allegations of bullying, harassment and sexual misconduct in the parliamentary community. Any adverse findings against an MP are reported to the Independent Expert Panel, which decides on the matter and recommends a suitable sanction if it upholds a complaint. It also provides for an appeal process on the decision and the sanction.

The Recall of MPs Act 2015 enables voters to launch an election petition demanding a by-election if an MP is given a custodial or suspended prison sentence of any length; or is suspended from the House for ten sitting days or fourteen calendar days or more, following a report by the Committee on Standards (or any other committee such as the Committee of Privileges charged with examining the conduct of an MP); or is convicted of providing false or misleading expenses claims. If 10 per cent of the registered voters in the seat sign the petition within six weeks, there is a by-election, in which the unseated MP can stand.

A statutory body, the Independent Parliamentary Standards Authority, has administered members' pay and business costs since 2012. By law it has a compliance officer charged with investigating complaints and irregularities.

Conduct in the chamber and in committee is the responsibility of the Speaker, or whoever is in the chair. In recent years the Speaker and Deputy Speakers have produced a booklet entitled *Rules of behaviour and courtesies in the House of Commons*. This includes advice on how to apply to speak in debates as well as rules on the use of electronic devices, parliamentary language, food and drink, proper attire and references to other members. Disorderly conduct such as waving the mace around or refusing to apologise for calling another member a liar, a rogue or dishonourable, can be punished immediately by the Speaker with a demand to physically withdraw from the chamber and the estate for the day or by an official 'naming', suspending a member for five sitting days.

Acknowledgements

My views on parliament and the need for reform have been framed over many years, but they have been refined thanks to the wisdom of all my colleagues on the Standards Committee, both past and present, so I am grateful to the lay members I have worked with, namely Rita Dexter, Jane Burgess, Tammy Banks, Paul Thorogood, Arun Midha, Mehmuda Mian, Victoria Smith, Michael Maguire, Sir Francis Habgood, David Stirling, Rose Marie Parr and Carys Williams; plus the MPs Sir Bernard Jenkin, Alberto Costa, Mark Fletcher, Andy Carter, Sir Charles Walker, Allan Dorans, Chris Elmore and Yvonne Fovargue. I have also been phenomenally fortunate to have been supported by some excellent clerks to the committee, namely Dr Robin James, Ben Street, Stuart Ramsey and Wafia Zia. All the good ideas are theirs, all the weaknesses in the argument are my own. Jonathan Evans, the chairman of the Committee on Standards in Public Life, has occasionally steered me back on to the strait and narrow and Christopher Geidt has provided sage counsel when I have needed it.

I have worked with two parliamentary commissioners for standards – Kathryn Stone OBE and Daniel Greenberg CB – so I know it is one of the most difficult jobs in modern political life. It requires discretion, a clear set of moral principles and a sense of proportion, but they have also had to draw on deep wells of personal fortitude at times. Together with the registrars of members' interests, Heather Wood and James Davies, and the senior investigations manager Helen Reid, they have performed an act of outstanding public service. I am grateful to them, as I hope is the whole of parliament.

Several colleagues helped by reading early drafts and suggesting improvements, including my longest-standing friend in parliament, Kevin Brennan, and the immensely wise Jess Phillips. Professor Meg Russell, the director of the Constitution Unit (which along with the Institute for Government has long laboured in the vineyard of better governance), also helped batter the section on corruption into a far better state than it started.

I am also indebted to many others who have written books on this topic, including Isabel Hardman's *Why We Get the Wrong Politicians*, Dorothy Byrne's *Trust Me, I'm Not a Politician*, Peter Oborne's *The Assault on Truth* and Hannah White's *Held in Contempt: What's Wrong with the House of Commons*.

My agent at United Agents, Jim Gill, and my editor at Bloomsbury, Jasmine Horsey, both encouraged me to write the book and assisted me immensely in delivering what I hope is a tight and well-informed contribution to the debate. Peter James and Francisco Vilhena as well as the rest of the Bloomsbury team have helped get the book ready in record time.

Above all, I am grateful to my colleagues in parliament who put up with my sanctimony, my office team (Gareth, Nataša, Geraint, Mark and Matthew) who admirably keep all the plates spinning, and my constituents in the Rhondda who have repeatedly returned me to parliament despite my manifest failings.

Notes

INTRODUCTION

1. House of Commons, Committee on Standards, *Mr Owen Paterson, Third Report of Session 2021–22*, HC 797, para. 212, p. 48
2. *Daily Telegraph*, 29 October 2021
3. HC, 30 October 1947, vol. 443, cols 1094–1228
4. HC, 3 November 2021, vol. 702, col. 905
5. Ibid., col. 938
6. Ibid., cols 960–4
7. House of Commons, Committee on Standards, *Mr Owen Paterson, Third Report of Session 2021–22*, HC 797, para. 212, p. 48
8. HC, 4 November 2021, vol. 702, col. 1054
9. HC, 16 November 2021, vol. 703, col. 476
10. Ibid., col. 480
11. https://www.ox.ac.uk/news/arts-blog/five-worst-parliaments-all-time
12. HC, 5 September 2019, vol. 664, col. 398
13. *Guardian*, 16 November 2022
14. https://news.sky.com/story/im-a-celebrity-rishi-sunak-suggests-matt-hancocks-appearance-is-not-noble-12748093
15. HC, 20 December 2022, vol. 725, col. 231
16. HC, 24 February 2023, vol. 728, col. 493
17. I also campaigned for it to be available online, which it now is. See https://erskinemay.parliament.uk

1 THE WORST PARLIAMENT IN HISTORY?

1. Independent Expert Panel, *Appeal by Andrew Bridgen MP*, HC 991, 20 December 2022
2. *Sun*, 1 December 2022
3. 'House of Commons Journal Volume 11: 22 January 1693' (1694 in modern dating), in *Journal of the House of Commons: Volume 11, 1693–1697* (London, 1803), p. 105
4. https://inews.co.uk/news/politics/end-booing-and-jeering-in-parliament-as-poll-shows-voters-lose-respect-for-politicians-when-watching-debates-1667928
5. HC, 22 January 2020, vol. 670, col. 292
6. HC, 11 January 2023, vol. 725, col. 559
7. HC, 7 December 2005, vol. 440, col. 861
8. *Argus*, 1 October 2019
9. https://www.newburytoday.co.uk/news/man-waged-campaign-of-terror-against-laura-farris-mp-9224442
10. 41 Geo. 3 ch. 63, s. 1
11. 33 & 34 Vict. ch. 91, s. 4
12. 'House of Commons Journal Volume 1: 2 March 1624', in *Journal of the House of Commons: Volume 1, 1547–1629* (London, 1802), p. 676
13. 'House of Commons Journal Volume 9: 30 December 1680', in *Journal of the House of Commons: Volume 9, 1667–1687* (London, 1802), p. 696
14. *Guardian*, 25 January 2011, p. 4
15. https://www.bbc.co.uk/news/uk-northern-ireland-12292896
16. 5 & 6 Eliz. 2. c. 24, s. 1

2 THE WINNER TAKES IT ALL

1. HC, 27 May 1886, vol. 306, col. 267
2. Daniel Mallory, ed., *The Life and Speeches of the Hon. Henry Clay*, Boston, R.P. Bixby & Company, 1843, p. 566
3. HC, 11 November 1947, vol. 444, col. 207

4. HC, 11 November 1947, vol. 444, cols 204–9

5. *Democracy Index 2022*, Economist Intelligence Unit, published 1 February 2023

6. HC, 1 April 2019, vol. 657, col. 814

7. The provision is in section 4(2)(d) and repeated at 4(5)(d)

8. HC, 16 April 2016, vol. 608, col. 668

9. HC, 22 October 2021, vol. 701, col. 1060

10. HC, 18 April 2016, vol. 608, col. 667

11. 'House of Commons Journal Volume 17: 11 June 1713', in *Journal of the House of Commons: Volume 17, 1711–1714* (London, 1803) p. 417. It is now incorporated in Standing Order 48 of the House of Commons

12. https://www.electoralcommission.org.uk/who-we-are-and-what-we-do/our-views-and-research/elections-act/a-strategy-and-policy-statement-electoral-commission

13. https://www.theguardian.com/media/greenslade/2015/mar/17/appeal-court-reduces-damages-award-against-sunday-times-to-50000

3 SOMETHING ROTTEN

1. https://www.bbc.co.uk/news/uk-politics-59238464

2. https://www.ft.com/content/1b4003fa-b179-4063-bfcb-2ee224b7a3fc

3. LBC, 5 December 2022

4. https://blogs.lse.ac.uk/politicsandpolicy/government-corruption

5. Ibid.

6. Ibid.

7. Findings of the Independent Adviser, Cabinet Office, 20 November 2020

8. Adam Tolley KC, *Formal Complaints about the Conduct of The Right Honourable Dominic Raab MP*, Cabinet Office, 2023, pp. 35, 45

9. https://www.transparency.org.uk/uk-politics-potential-ministerial-code-breaches

10. Committee on Standards in Public Life, *Upholding Standards in Public Life 2021*, para 4.25

11. https://registrarofconsultantlobbyists.org.uk/summary-of-investigation-the-rt-hon-owen-paterson-mr-paterson

12. HC, 8 December 2022, vol. 724, col. 521

13. The Ministerial Code can be found here: https://www.gov.uk/government/publications/ministerial-code

14. HC, 22 June 2022, vol. 716, col. 845

15. HC, 26 October 2021, vol. 702, col. 139

16. Erskine May Online, para. 7.31. https://erskinemay.parliament.uk/section/6479/opposed-returns/

17. *The Code of Conduct*, HC1083, p. 12, para.14 and p. 17 para. 17(j)

18. Committee on Standards, *Oral Evidence: Code of Conduct Consultation*, HC 954, Q474, 26 April 2022

19. https://www.thetimes.co.uk/article/boris-johnson-and-the-multimillionaire-canadian-cousin-who-lent-a-hand-qzcf2m7jp

20. HC, 12 December 2022, vol. 724, col. 823. She also said 'as we head into summer' in the same debate

21. HC, 16 July 2018, vol. 645, col. 33

22. *The Tier 1 (Investor) route, Written Statement made on 12 January 2023*, UIN HCWS492

23. *The Times*, 22 April 2022

24. https://www.bbc.co.uk/news/uk-54228079

25. https://www.bbc.co.uk/news/uk-politics-61080537

26. https://www.bbc.co.uk/news/uk-54228079

27. https://www.theguardian.com/politics/2022/dec/21/honours-committees-pressured-by-no-10-to-reward-tory-donors

28. https://www.theguardian.com/politics/2022/feb/19/six-tory-donors-given-top-cultural-posts-since-boris-johnson-became-pm

29. The Seven Principles of Public Life, Committee on Standards in Public Life, 31 May 1995, https://www.gov.uk/government/publications/the-7-principles-of-public-life/the-7-principles-of-public-life--2

30. https://www.transparency.org/en/what-is-corruption
31. HL, 13 October 2022, vol. 824, col. 164GC
32. HC, 25 March 2021, vol. 691, col. 1045
33. https://www.bmj.com/content/376/bmj.o96
34. https://www.theguardian.com/politics/2022/jan/12/use-of-vip-lane-to-award-covid-ppe-contracts-unlawful-high-court-rules
35. https://www.theguardian.com/politics/2021/nov/16/michael-gove-backer-won-164m-in-ppe-contracts-after-vip-lane-referral
36. https://www.opendemocracy.net/en/dark-money-investigations/record-profits-for-firm-involved-in-bungled-250m-ppe-deal
37. https://www.bbc.co.uk/news/uk-england-suffolk-59521231
38. https://www.theguardian.com/politics/2023/feb/12/firm-won-ppe-contract-greg-hands-approached-by-tory-activist-luxe-lifestyle
39. https://www.spotlightcorruption.org/half-of-vip-lane-companies-supplied-ppe-worth-1-billion-that-was-not-fit-for-purpose
40. HC, 22 February 2021, vol. 689, col. 634
41. https://www.theguardian.com/uk-news/2022/nov/23/revealed-tory-peer-michelle-mone-secretly-received-29m-from-vip-lane-ppe-firm
42. It is available online here: https://www.parliament.uk/business/publications/house-of-lords-publications/rules-and-guides-for-business/companion-to-the-standing-orders
43. https://www.gov.uk/government/collections/towns-fund
44. https://committees.parliament.uk/publications/3373/documents/32489/default
45. https://www.gov.uk/government/publications/levelling-up-fund-round-2-prospectus/levelling-up-fund-round-2-prospectus
46. https://committees.parliament.uk/publications/22483/documents/165800/default
47. *Manchester Evening News*, 20 January 2022

48. Public Administration and Constitutional Affairs Committee, Oral Evidence: The Work of the Cabinet Office, 20 January 2022, HC41, Q92

4 THE WORST LIES IN LONDON

1. HC, 1 December 2021, vol. 704, col. 909; 8 December 2021, vol. 705, col. 372; ibid.; 8 December 2021, vol. 705, col. 379
2. HC, 21 April 2022, vol. 712, col. 426
3. https://uksa.statisticsauthority.gov.uk/correspondence/sir-david-norgrove-to-prime-minister-employment-statistics
4. Liaison Committee, *Oral evidence: Evidence from the Prime Minister*, 30 March 2022, HC 1211, Q77
5. https://www.gov.uk/government/speeches/prime-minister-boris-johnsons-statement-in-downing-street-7-july-2022
6. HC, 30 November 2022, vol. 723, col. 896
7. HC, 6 January 2022, vol. 706, col. 160
8. Department for Health and Social Care, Consultation document: changes to Human Medicine Regulations to support the rollout of COVID-19 vaccines
9. *Guardian*, 2 December 2020
10. https://ourworldindata.org/coronavirus
11. HC, 19 March 1997, vol. 292, col. 1047
12. Written evidence submitted to the Procedure Committee Inquiry on Correcting the Record, by Professor Meg Russell, Director, Constitution Unit, UCL (CTR 08), 24 November 2022
13. *Guide to Parliamentary Work*, Cabinet Office, p. 61
14. Procedure Committee, *Oral evidence: Correcting the record*, HC 521, Wednesday 19 October 2022, Q1
15. House of Commons Library
16. HC, 9 November 2022, vol. 722, col. 254
17. *Clarification, Statement made on 23 February 2022*, Statement UIN HCWS627

18. Department of Health and Social Care, New Hospital Programme Fact Sheet. https://healthmedia.blog.gov. uk/2023/05/25/new-hospital-programme-media-fact-sheet/

19. https://erskinemay.parliament.uk/section/4874/language-and-allegations-in-relation-to-other-members-and-members-of-the-house-of-lords

20. HC, 13 June 2012, vol. 546, cols 344–5

21. HC, 21 April 2022, vol. 712, col. 351

22. The Culture Committee said, 'We are disappointed that despite being provided with several opportunities to reconsider her position, the former Secretary of State failed to countenance that her recollections may have been flawed. People will be able to draw their own conclusions about the contrast between her claims and subsequent correspondence with the committee, and Channel 4's thorough investigation'

23. https://www.huffingtonpost.co.uk/2012/03/05/politicians-lie-all-the-time-peter-kellner-yougov-poll_n_1320286.html

24. https://www.electoralcalculus.co.uk/blogs/ec_mpstandards_20210422.html; https://yougov.co.uk/topics/politics/articles-reports/2022/04/21/eight-10-britons-say-boris-johnson-lied-about-lock

25. https://www.ucl.ac.uk/constitution-unit/sites/constitution_unit/files/report_1_final_digital.pdf; https://www.ucl.ac.uk/constitution-unit/sites/constitution_unit/files/ucl_cu_report3_digital_final.pdf; *What Kind of Democracy Do People Want?* (pub. 2022) and *Public Preferences for Integrity and Accountability in Politics* (pub. 2023), Constitution Unit

26. https://www.parliament.uk/globalassets/investigation-report-for-19-october-2022.pdf

27. Attributed to Jowett in Edwin Milton Royle's *Peace and Quiet: A Novel*, London, Harper & Brothers, 1916

28. *The Times*, 28 January 2023

29. HC, 14 June 2021, vol. 697, col. 21

30. The original comment is at HC, 14 December 2021, vol. 705, col. 968. The correction is at HC, 8 February 2022, vol. 708, col. 916

31. https://fullfact.org/about/policy/reports/full-fact-report-2023/report

32. Digital, Culture, Media and Sport Committee, Sub-committee on Online Harms and Disinformation, *Oral evidence: Misinformation and trusted voices*, 29 November 2022, HC597

33. HC, 17 June 2021, vol. 697, col. 436

34. HC, 14 November 2022, vol. 722, col. 424

35. HC, 1 February 2017, vol. 620, col. 1076

36. Committee of Privileges Oral evidence: Matter referred on 21 April 2022: Conduct of Rt Hon Boris Johnson MP, HC 564, Wednesday 22 March 2023, Q41

37. Privileges Committee, Matter referred on 21 April 2022 (conduct of Rt Hon Boris Johnson): Final Report, 15 June 2023, para. 229. https://committees.parliament.uk/publications/40412/documents/197199/default

5   CONDUCT UNBECOMING

1. HC, 3 December 1953, vol. 521, col. 1298

2. HC, 13 February 1989, vol. 147, col. 25

3. Written Evidence submitted to the Speaker's Conference on employment of MPs' staff (SPC0015), https://committees.parliament.uk/writtenevidence/113051/html/

4. HC, 20 April 1911, vol. 24, col. 1112

5. Randolph S. Churchill, *Winston Churchill: Young Statesman, 1901–1914*, London, Heinemann, 1967, p. 344

6. https://www.politico.eu/article/uk-mps-parliament-appg-house-of-commons-accused-of-using-foreign-trips-for-sex-tourism

7. See the evidence submitted by the unions to the Speaker's conference on employment of MPs' staff.

8. The Speaker's Conference, Written evidence submitted by the GMB, SPC0016

9. https://www.newstatesman.com/politics/uk-politics/2023/01/exclusive-lee-anderson-mp-staff-turnover

10. *A House for Everyone: A Case for Modernising Parliament*, Fawcett Society, 2023. https://www.fawcettsociety.org.uk/a-house-for-everyone

11. House of Commons Library

12. https://www.parliament.uk/globalassets/mps-lords--offices/standards-and-financial-interests/independent-expert-panel/hc-12---the-conduct-of-mr-mike-hill.pdf

13. Independent Expert Panel, *The Conduct of Mr Patrick Grady MP*, HC 368

14. Independent Expert Panel, *The Conduct of Mr Christian Matheson MP*, HC 823

15. https://www.tortoisemedia.com/audio/a-finding-of-rape/

16. *Daily Mail*, 9 February 2023

6 CONFLICT OF INTEREST

1. HC, 1 May 2018, vol. 640, cols 183, 189, 226

2. https://hansard.parliament.uk/commons/2018-05-01/debates/9BE03BAC-2539-4951-88A2-9A8A20D7A1A3/SanctionsAndAnti-MoneyLaunderingBill(Lords); https://www.theguardian.com/politics/2021/nov/10/geoffrey-cox-faces-conflict-of-interest-claim-in-uk-parliament

3. https://www.gov.uk/government/publications/british-virgin-islands-commission-of-inquiry-report/british-virgin-islands-commission-of-inquiry-report-executive-summary

4. Email to the author, 5 May 2023

5. The Code of Conduct, p. 11

6. https://www.ipsos.com/en-uk/half-britons-disapprove-mps-having-second-jobs-it-depends-what-job

7. Labour Party, *A New Britain: Renewing our Democracy and Rebuilding our Economy*, 2022, p. 130

8. HC, 17 November 2021, vol. 703, col. 635

9. Committee on Standards in Public Life, *MPs' Outside Interests*, July 2018, recommendation 1

10. *Daily Mail*, 16 November 2021

11. *Guardian*, 14 January 2006

12. Standards Committee, *Nadine Dorries, Fourth Report of Session 2013–14*, HC806

13. https://www.youtube.com/watch?v=UswbkeyGDLU

14. https://www.parliament.uk/globalassets/documents/pcfs/advice-notes/advice-note-2023.03.16---paid-parliamentary-advice.pdf

15. Sir Thomas Cooke, Henry Guy, Thomas Coulson, Sir Edward Seymour, Sir Samuel Dashwood, Henry Goldwell, Sir John Fleet, John Perry, Sir Joseph Herne and Sir Basil Firebrace (of whom a contemporary wrote, the 'noted old sinner of London, has shot himself, but 'tis thought 'twill not prove mortal, as some perhaps could wish, whom he had cheated by odd tricks and shams, from whence he grew rich')

16. 'House of Commons Journal Volume 11: 2 May 1695', in *Journal of the House of Commons: Volume 11, 1693–1697* (London, 1803), p. 331

17. HC, 20 April 1995, vol. 258, col. 356

18. Select Committee on Standards and Privileges *Seventh Report of 1997–98 Session*, https://publications.parliament.uk/pa/cm199798/cmselect/cmstnprv/240vii/sp0703.htm

19. *Daily Telegraph*, 8 February 2010

20. https://www.appgbusinessresilience.org/; https://www.cignpost.com/

21. https://www.appghousing.org.uk

22. https://www.tendoconsulting.co.uk/

7 HELPING OURSELVES

1. https://yougov.co.uk/topics/politics/articles-reports/2021/12/17/john-humphrys-are-our-politicians-worst-ever

2. HC, 30 June 2016, vol. 612, cols 467–8

3. Cited by Theresa May, HC, 20 February 2019, vol. 654, col. 1457

4. HC, 17 June 1963, vol. 679, col. 54

Index

A Note on the Author

Chris Bryant is an award-winning historian of Parliament and an expert on parliamentary procedure. Having been MP for the Rhondda since 2001, he has since 2020 chaired the Committees on Standards and Privileges, which have guardianship of the Code of Conduct and adjudicate on individual cases. He won the *Spectator* Speech of the Year award in 2021 for his calm exposition of the case against Owen Paterson and has drafted the new House of Commons Code of Conduct.